For more than two decades, Helen Razer has been broadcasting and writing her way into disagreement of various scales. She has been employed as a contributor by *The Age* and *The Australian*, and is now a columnist on dissent with *Crikey* and gardening correspondent for *The Saturday Paper*. Helen has produced four previous books of humorous non-fiction and her frequently published thoughts on the impotence of current public debate are extended in *A Short History of Stupid*, co-authored with her friend and colleague Bernard Keane.

By the same author

A Short History of Stupid

HELEN RAZER

THE HELEN 100

HOW I TOOK MY WAXER'S ADVICE AND CURED HEARTBREAK BY GOING ON 100 DATES IN LESS THAN A YEAR

ALLEN&UNWIN
SYDNEY・MELBOURNE・AUCKLAND・LONDON

First published in 2017

Copyright © Helen Razer 2017

All rights reserved. No part of this book may be reproduced or transmitted in any form or by any means, electronic or mechanical, including photocopying, recording or by any information storage and retrieval system, without prior permission in writing from the publisher. The Australian *Copyright Act 1968* (the Act) allows a maximum of one chapter or 10 per cent of this book, whichever is the greater, to be photocopied by any educational institution for its educational purposes provided that the educational institution (or body that administers it) has given a remuneration notice to the Copyright Agency (Australia) under the Act.

Many identifying details have been changed to preserve the privacy of all individuals depicted. All the names have been changed, save for mine and my cat's. (And those of Bradley Cooper and Karl Marx. Obviously.)

Allen & Unwin
83 Alexander Street
Crows Nest NSW 2065
Australia
Phone: (61 2) 8425 0100
Email: info@allenandunwin.com
Web: www.allenandunwin.com

Cataloguing-in-Publication details are available
from the National Library of Australia
www.trove.nla.gov.au

ISBN 978 1 74331 828 7

Set in 12/18 pt Sabon LT by Midland Typesetters, Australia
Printed and bound in Australia by Griffin Press

10 9 8 7 6 5 4 3 2 1

MIX
Paper from responsible sources
FSC® C009448

The paper in this book is FSC® certified. FSC® promotes environmentally responsible, socially beneficial and economically viable management of the world's forests.

1

Forty-eight hours and one shower since she left
'Dolphin,' said Eleni, my waxer of some years.

In the language of Eleni's salon, 'to dolphin' is to turn left on a table with the rear thrust out while lying naked from the bottom down. It's a short and useful command that, once learned, urges the lady to an ideal position for a brief 'bikini' wax. It also has the psychological effect of sanitising the client's vagina and her cruder neighbour, the anus. To believe for a moment that one's most abject parts resemble Flipper's mouth is quite relaxing.

But this was not a likeness noted by Eleni, whose long professional scrutiny of female anuses through a magnifying lamp certainly qualified her to make such comparisons. Apparently, we ladies do not look like dolphins Down There;

probably, if we're using marine life as a guide, more like a mollusc. However, on the wall Eleni's anal-waxees were required to face, there happened to be a promotional poster for a moisturising gel that depicted a well-hydrated dolphin. Hence Eleni had developed the 'Dolphin!' command.

I laughed, as I always do, and I seized, as I frequently do, the fleshiest part of one buttock and moved it up and down, emitting 'eEeEeEeEeEeEeEeE eEeEeEeEeEeEeEeE,' from my mouth. Eleni said she was relieved that I was making my customarily crap jokes, and, again, how *very* sorry she was that she had waxed my ex's anus that one quite recent time.

'I should have charged her double. I saw all the hair she had down there and asked, "Are you Greek like me?" I don't think it was very nice of her to wait so long for me to wax it. I used more than half a pot.'

Not that I had minded when the ex's bush had recalled a goliath tarantula. Not that I had minded its fashionable deforestation. It was quite a nice vagina either way. But, right now, I *did* mind thinking about my ex's sexual parts in any way at all, and tailored to my grief as Eleni's observations were— among them, 'I used enough wax on that thing to cover a truck full of Babybel cheeses'—I asked her to desist.

I told Eleni that I couldn't bear to talk about the tarantula again, and asked if we could *please* change the topic from my tragic break-up.

I then immediately resumed the topic of my tragic break-up—it hurts *so much*, my longest intimacy has *ended*, my ex had turned to hairless sex with other women like a duck to orange sauce, etc.—and continued right until the moment hot wax made its way toward my rectum.

'Was that warmer than usual?' I asked Eleni.

'No,' she lied, and she tore me a new arsehole, to bear in this parched Melbourne summer.

Eleni is a very sweet person who generally brings the same care to conversation she does to the removal of hair from my anal cleft. But that day she'd likely had her fill of my outpourings, which had already drenched a manicure, an eyebrow tint and a mini facial—a service she had offered, as she does to all newly dumped clients with puffy eyes, on-the-house.

'I know you are sad, Helen. And I am happy to listen to you talk about some of it. But words can be dangerous. It does you no good to use them all the time.'

And, I imagine that it did Eleni no good to tend to my vagina while I banged on about how it had been so newly vacated, so I tried to address a topic that wasn't my dolphin, or the ex's dolphin, but failed. For a moment, I forewent the futile ecstasy of most words by uttering that actually useful one, 'sorry'. And then I would return to useless words again.

2

Six hours and one chicken since she left

Two days before the dolphin, I had been quite atypically wordless. Those sounds with my mouth I had managed to make owed less to spoken English than they did to the language of the abattoir. 'Mooooargheeow,' I said, or something very like it, and when I echoed the complaint of the doomed heifer, I reminded myself to become a vegetarian should I ever again decide to eat.

Eleven the cat had managed to retain his carnivorous appetites, notwithstanding the awful thing that had just happened to both of us. So, shortly after the ex had declared herself the ex, I ordered him a home-delivered chicken by telephone. Finding the words to achieve this was trying, but not quite so trying as I imagined operation of the can-opener would prove. Newly dumped people are as capable with kitchen tools as they are with words.

Public Service Announcement: The newly dumped should stay away from any device more complex or more dangerous than a spork.

A man of very belligerent cheer delivered the chicken. 'Here's a tasty chook for a tasty lady!' he said, lying on both counts. I tore it into small pieces and I told Eleven a few things as he ate it. Among them, 'I don't mind if you eat me when I die,' and, 'Your other mummy is a whore.'

Not that he minded. Eleven was as happy with this divorce as a cat could be—which is, of course, obscenely so. His eyes had closed when I pulled apart the first greaseproof bag and did not open fully again for days. His purr was violent, his bliss extreme, and he stared at me through his furry cat-lids and said, 'We will live here on the floor with our barbecue chickens. Forever.'

One day, animal behaviourists will confirm what feline companions already know: cats are the covert architects of human emotional crisis. I have never known a domestic cat that did not thrive on hominid despair. Eleven had always quite liked me, but never so much as when I was a jilted, masturbating wreck, whose needy petting larded his tabby fur with a film of chicken fat. 'You had a paw in this, didn't you?' I said to him, and he crawled onto my shoulders and planed at my grief with his sandpaper.

No one told me the end of a fifteen-year relationship would smell exactly like barbecue chicken, but this would be misery's signature scent. When my partner had gone, I fell with a chicken to the floor.

She had not said very much before she left. She had said, 'I'm leaving you', 'I need to grow' and 'Things have been bad for a while'. Apparently, her faculty for speech had packed up and left minutes before she did.

'I need to grow' was shocking but also quite familiar. I'd never had such a shop-worn break-up statement addressed directly to me, but I'd certainly heard similar things in television dramas or in accounts by others. 'He said to me, "It's not you, it's me." Can you believe that?' people would say, and *no*, I never really could.

I had been *told* that absconding spouses tell standard lies when remarkable lies are needed, but I'd never supposed it could actually be true.

What I had supposed was that when dumped people recounted dialogue from their break-ups, they did so through memory's unreliable filter. *Surely* no one actually *says* this shit. *Surely*, the people who think that they have heard these hackneyed things have simply misremembered. *Surely*, fugitive spouses are so adrenalised before they run out the door, they have something more interesting to say than 'I need to grow' or 'I really need more space'.

Of course, it's not as if my first responses—'Let's grow together!', 'I'll give you more space!' and 'Well, fuck you in your slut hole, then!'—had recalled the choicest of Dorothy Parker. Talking shit when someone leaves you, however, is fairly defensible. Talking shit when you're leaving someone else is absolutely not.

I need to grow. The phrase 'I need to grow' is a weapon of such deadly banality, it should be declared illegal. That so many small crimes are harshly penalised while this one goes unpunished suggests that our lawmakers are philandering pricks who, at one point or another, have all 'needed to grow'. Probably deep inside some voluptuous administrator who has been freshly dolphined.

I have never left a spouse and, given my aversion to packing boxes and redirecting mail, it is very unlikely that I will. But, if such horror unfolds, I vow it will be preceded by a wonderful speech.

Years ago, I saw a friend's then-husband talk at the funeral for a well-known writer. He spoke powerfully and weaved a little Auden into the eulogy—not the 'Stop all the Clocks' poem everybody-and-their-barking-dog now dies to but one written for Yeats. 'The words of a dead man are modified in the guts of the living,' he said.

He spoke very well at the funeral for his eminent friend, whose words I still digest. At the funeral for his marriage, though, he didn't bother with inspiring poetry. He just said, 'I need to grow.'

And this is what she said to me. Actually, she didn't *say* 'I need to grow', but wrote it down and sent it by Facebook message from across the house:

This is over. I don't think we're good for each other and things have been bad for a while. I'm leaving you because I need to grow.

I would say that at this point 'the floor fell away'. However, such description is hazardous to the health of the newly dumped; a needy demographic and one to whom this account of my own dump recovery is entirely dedicated. Chestnuts of the 'I need to grow' variety are likely to bring you poor dumped sods out in an allergic rash. So, instead I shall just say that I was very dizzy. The floor didn't fall away, but I fell on it, and remained there almost without pause until I was prompted by desire two days later to 'dolphin' and to date. A questionable program of recovery I will, as I said, soon describe.

I was on the floor as Eleven ate his chicken. He ate the corpse of the bird with ten times the relish I imagined he would later visit upon mine. I saw myself dead on this floor. My lifeless hand, still resting on the Romantic Drama section of the Netflix app, was not even chewed to the bone. 'She didn't taste good enough to eat,' said the coroner's report. 'There was nothing for this woman between break-up and death. She was modified in the guts of a tabby.'

Was there ever any other hope, though? Was I ever *not* going to be half-eaten by the cat as Jerry Maguire gave his dreadful speech about compassionate business? Perhaps the ex was right. Perhaps things *had* been bad for a while, because if they had not been bad, then my filthy, tangled, chicken-scented hair would not now be stuck between the floorboards.

I looked at my hair resting in the grooves between the floorboards and I tried to recall the last date on which it had been brushed. Or washed. I could not. I reasoned that there was little point in caring for it now—*obviously*, I was going to die, be partially eaten and then inadequately memorialised. But I did concede that I might not now be *quite* so close to death had I recently seen to my hair.

I should have brushed my hair. I should have done my nails. I should have taken the best advice of all marriage manuals and not worn elasticised waistbands in the company of my spouse. I had worn elasticised waistbands for months and for months. I had been tolerably miserable.

This misery and poor costume was partly down to her, partly down to me, but largely, I think, down to labour, which had been with an online discount advertiser.

The pay was not the worst that I've received, but the labour itself was horrifying—and I say this as a former cold-call sales associate who peddled low-document, high-interest loans to poor people over the phone during dinner. Now, following the predatory lending gig, I worked for a low-prestige advertising company and I had found myself in middle-income hell.

There are few enterprises worse than lending; the practice is actually wicked. But I had been happier truly knowing that I worked for the devil than merely suspecting it. And I suspected it often in this feel-good fun factory where employees were not just required to produce peppy 100-word lies about particular cut-rate beauty services but to actively participate in the lie that this work was fun. Fun!

The style guide at this company urged for overuse of exclamation points and Capital Letters. It requested 'pun-filled, fun-filled Aspirational Paragraphs for our on-fleek, AB MilleniGals!' Roughly translated, this describes 'shitty jokes that contain social media slang aimed at white women still young enough to access their wealthy parents' credit cards.'

The writers' room held toy boxes filled with Lego and other developmental playthings that, I had been told, would help us all rebuild our childlike sense of fun. Fun! Once a week, the building elevator was fitted with a camera and we were encouraged to record our 'very best hopes and dreams'. Every Friday the company renamed the elevator The Optimitorium.

I do not know if 'Optimitorium' refers to optimism or optimisation, or both, or nothing. And I do not fucking care. But I did care that this compulsory whimsy nourished little in me but despair.

Fun!

This work was not fun. But it might have been *almost* tolerable if some frisky bint called Brynlee hadn't cantered about in raw denim screeching, 'Dixie has totally *nailed* her deep-nourishing keratin treatment copy and is now in the running to be Australia's Next Top Social Advertising Model! Yay, Dixie! Fun!' whenever copy production rates were down.

Which they often were, due to widespread workplace abuse of Xanax, the only legal means to muffle the sound of Brynlee.

After a few months of motivational team talks, exclamation points and Lego, I became anxious enough to consult the discount psychologist, Gerard. When I told Cheap Gerard that I sometimes felt like I was on the devil's payroll, he suggested I speak with a priest. I suspect that Cheap Gerard is either a very good Catholic or a very poor listener who doesn't know metaphorical shorthand when he hears it. Still, I took his advice and spoke with a local priest one lunchtime.

The priest turned out to be a pretty decent bloke. He said that he, like me, doubted the existence of a material devil, but that he did believe in the metaphoric power of 2 Corinthians 11 to explain the character of an advertising company full of insincerely happy people: *For such are false apostles, deceitful workers, transforming themselves into the apostles of Christ. And no wonder, for Satan himself masquerades as an angel of light.*

He told me I was right to feel that this is false gospel that preaches for the father of poisonous lies. 'There is nothing that is not deceitful about telling women they are ugly and imperfect to make them part with money,' he said, which was a lot more feminism than one anticipates from Mother Church.

'There is nothing that is not evil about pretending that this work is good for its producers and consumers,' he said, which was a lot more communism that one anticipates from Mother Church.

The sensible Father counselled me to leave the agency, but hang on to its wage. 'Since you can't get your job back with the terrible phone-loans people since they were shut down for fraud, you might want to ask Brynlee if you could work from home.'

I accepted his advice, and his gift of a Pope Francis portrait.

Brynlee, whose eyes often fixed me with the sort of fearful disgust otherwise set on the nutrition labels of high-carbohydrate snacks, quickly agreed to my departure. People like me, with inclination for neither whimsy nor Lego, troubled her. She said I could 'satellite' on the condition that I increase my exclamation point quota and compose at least a dozen promotional coupons for Crypto-Satan every day. These were to be 'like, totally *brainy*' for the company's direct targeting of well-to-do arts undergraduates from the nation's better universities. I was to include frequent and obvious references to the best-known phrases in out-of-copyright English literature and/or popular culture.

> If every face tells a story, then let the lines of yours be gone sooner than a sonnet! Hydro-micro-dermabrasion is Poetically Proven to reduce the signs of looking unlovelier than a summer's day! For just $39.99! That's 66% off! Discounts like these shake the darling buds of cray . . .

. . . is just the sort of thing Brynlee enjoyed receiving from me twelve times a day.

Fun!

As it turned out, you can't write this shit at speed in uncomfortable pants. And you can't write this shit every day and not begin to loathe yourself and the lies that you've been selling.

Each morning, in my elasticised pants, I downloaded the job orders for tooth-whitening or fat-reducing or hair-straightening deals, and each afternoon I would be almost dead with hate. I could hardly bear to sell this stuff and I lived by not buying it at all. I didn't just renounce the particular products and services I was selling but, gradually, the entire idea of personal grooming.

I found that I had to keep on giving up *something* to maintain productivity. Committing such a sin seemed to demand regular sacrifice. I'd renounced the company of others. I'd renounced my ambition to write anything of value ever again—not that I ever *had* produced words of value, but the conceit I was wasting my gifts had previously brought me pleasure. I'd even, in visiting a priest, momentarily renounced my aversion to religion; an aversion which, as is the case with many atheists, had itself become a bit religious. This was my Lent in reverse.

I had renounced nearly everything in the attempt to remain alive. I was in danger of renouncing the means to live altogether, and the day I got an order to sell something called 'frizz ensmoothenation' was the day I knew I could either tell this work, and all work, to go and fuck itself or give up on brushing my hair.

And now the hair whose care was one of the last things I had left to renounce was stuck with chicken grease to the grooves between my floorboards.

That morning, before the ex left, I had been assigned a job for a Thai breast enlargement treatment. I always found Asian-themed jobs particularly trying because it took forever to think my way out of the obvious orientalism. My colleagues would quickly write things like 'exotic' and 'mystical' and 'spicy', and even though we were all working together in the service of cut-rate vanity, this didn't mean I had to give up *all* my hopes for decent society. Markdown manipulation of women who hated their bodies by clumsy theft of the most beautiful verse in English was bad enough, but I didn't have to be a colonial arsehole with it.

I had been struggling for an hour to not be a racist with the natural Thai breast enlargement: a procedure that apparently involved being hit in the tits with a stick. But the production of advertising copy, even this low-rent kind, was something I usually found difficult. Every word has a commercial weight and I had to almost feel it in the palm of my hand before I set it on the page.

It was then, between these breasts, that the ex slapped me with the news that she was leaving me.

When she had left, I sat at my computer, with the breast enlargement on it, and suddenly it became easy to violate developing nations. I promised vain, small-breasted white women sexy oriental secrets. I may have used the terms 'concubine' and 'geisha' in my One Size Fits Most approach to the great continent of Asia. I don't recall exactly what *memsaab* shit I upchucked that day and I do not care at all to remember. But I do know that I wrote twenty to one hundred Brynlee coupons, each freer from ethics than the last.

Who wants to be fat? Who wants to look old? Who wants to pay full price to Asians for a gel polish manicure?

It's quite easy for your ethics not to matter when nothing matters at all. Of course I now feel terrible about using the phrase 'mystic East', but I was eventually grateful for this rush as it turned out to be my last act of money-making in months. My time would not be spent in service to productivity but to grief and to dating and my dolphin.

I ordered my first barbecue chicken. I lay miserable and godless on the floor. I dispatched one last discount beauty coupon, and when I did that I gave in utterly to the flash of chaos that always comes when we know that love is gone.

At about ten that night, I emailed:

Dear Brynlee,

I am slashing my services to your organisation by 100%. This is due in part to the recent departure of all my childlike wonder, which pulled out of the driveway in a Toyota sedan at 4 p.m.

It is also due to my revulsion for exclamation points! I know it is the view of the company that these signify fun to consumers, but I believe they suggest evidence of a dangerous personality disorder. And the risk of death by torture! In a basement! Do you know any functionally sane person who uses more than one exclamation point per correspondence per year? No! You don't! There is a reason that we moved only three units of frizz ensmoothenation last month and it's not because straight hair has lost its cultural appeal in this horrid, racist nation that valorises the flat and the white. It is because you compel me to produce terrifying schizotypal copy that serves more as a warning of murder than it does an inducement to buy.

These things we write are not mere advertisements. These are ugly ransom notes that threaten their recipient with the slaughter of the soul. We kidnap and confine their confidence. They agree to pay half-price for its partial return.

Only a MilleniGal who has had the dignity fucked out of her by a concrete dildo could continue to do this work of Satan, Brynlee. I have never been sadder nor more distressed in any professional environment, and I once sold sub-prime mortgages to impoverished persons from a building that smelled like a cage of sick mice. That your bleak and often evil work is done with lashings of team spirit has truly eaten my guts. 'Fun' office environments such as yours perpetually promise freedom, but perpetually deliver its very opposite.

Don't pretend to promise freedom, Brynlee. Better for me, and for all of us, the diabolic manager who rages 'Schnell! Schnell!' than your false, empowered prophet. Every time you told me I was free, or that our customers were, it hurt me.

It is too late for me, Brynlee. My insides are dead. But, you are young and can still redeem yourself. If you do not run from them now, Daily Deals will steal the stuff of you, too.

Please find my terminal invoice herewith.

I wrote the note, fed little Eleven again and thought for one to four hours that night about brushing and cleaning my hair, if only in readiness for death. Which was the only kind of plan that had formed thus far from a mean and greasy floor.

3

Nine hours and no libidinal relief since she left
Like many who find themselves wearing elasticised pants in front of their spouses, I had not had sex in some time. I hadn't wanted sex in some time. By 9 p.m. that night, though, I absolutely did. I wanted sex. I just wanted sex. I mean, *really* wanted it, like older men report their teenaged selves having wanted it.

I felt like a delivery truck packed with full-fat yoghurt that would crash if not unloaded. And I apologise for the inelegance of this image. But, as I have said, this is an account intended chiefly for use by the newly dumped and they are, for good reason, terribly sensitive about the use of cliché. So, I'm hardly going to say in front of them, 'I was forcefully seized by desire', am I?

Wanting sex, I have since learned, is a fairly standard middle-class female response to the shock of separation. I believe it comes a close second to going to Italy and Finding Oneself. I know this, because I texted my friend Celine, who is the only person I could count on to say something absurd instead of something sentimental.

Helen: So, very serious dispatch. 1. I've just been properly dumped and she's gone for good and I don't know why and I'm devastated. 2. I am totally gagging for sex, but also crying. What even is that?

Celine: First, I never liked the bint and if I were lez, I would totes do you, you have great tits, so fuck her. Second, this post-dump state is so common, it even has a name: Divorce Horn.

I tried to honk it that night.

If you are neither biologically old enough to be my parent nor young enough to be my issue, I cordially invite you to my muff.

I wrote this on a smutty corner of the internet and was not, unsurprisingly, inundated with responses until I added a picture of my tits, which are, as Celine will confirm, quite good, even in stressful conditions.

But even post-tit picture, finding sex by internet wasn't as easy as ordering a chicken. It was difficult for several reasons, some of which may be fairly universal, one of which is specific to those with a particular character flaw: some of us just don't have the faculty for daydreams. I shall review this problem, which actually has no solution, first. You may find it, to employ a dreadful term our Brynlee overused, 'relatable'.

There are some folks like me who don't dare to dream because we really can't. Our imaginations suffer from practical interference. If we try to enjoy, say, thoughts of lottery winnings, we can't go straight to fantasy spending on penthouses or, say, artisanal cheese.

Before we get to the make-believe money, we perform tedious accounting. Answering the question 'What would YOU do if you won the Powerball?' is not relaxing for me but a pain in my arse. I feel obliged to calculate how much of this imaginary $3.5M sum I must use for taxation, charitable donation, and behavioural therapy, all of which I imagine are outlays urgently needed upon receipt of an unusually large cheque.

So, I don't buy lottery tickets. I don't imagine becoming friends with famous people I am unlikely to meet. I also find it difficult to enjoy fantasy stories in general, especially those about sexy vampires. I once heard that vampires, in which I do not believe, are averse to running water, which means they would find it nearly impossible to bathe. As I did for some days following this shock separation.

As I sat with my phone, working up a sour summertime dolphin, I began to think of all the things that were just as unlikely as me getting sex. I thought about the impossibility of world peace when I saw a XXX profile that included some of the lyrics to John Lennon's 'Imagine'. I wrote to its author:

MuffDiva: To imagine all the people living life in peace and in no countries is to assume a utopian position ignorant of the birth of the nation-state. It is to forget that we remain aggressors in an ongoing war outside our borders. It is to overlook the thousands of brown bodies that were burned in the desert last week. And these are memories I cannot erase, as I had a high school history teacher called Mr Dean who made me learn about the importance of remembering history.

She is yet to reply.

I should say that Mr Dean gave me an F for history as I was, at the time, smoking a lot of weed and submitting essays rich in idiocy. But he was a very decent teacher who provided, despite my opposition, good grounding in international relations. I learned from him that one cannot simply wish history away. I learned that crying 'I don't understand how this evil could possibly happen' in response to a tragedy of war is lazy bullshit. You *can* understand how it happened, if only you look to the past.

So now when I hear 'Imagine', I always think, Fuck you, John Lennon. You were eating cheese in your penthouse when you wrote that oblivious dirge.

If you are, like me, the sort of person who cannot think of world peace without considering the problem of history, or of the lottery without therapists, or of vampires without soap, then you are the sort of person who cannot easily think that sex will unfold at 2 a.m. And I know there are certain Brynlees who recommend 'visualising' one's future. But, as we know, these people have had their brains fucked out by concrete dildos.

In short, I thought too much, and I imagine that even for the competent daydreamer, this is a fairly usual just-dumped problem.

Public Service Announcement: Try not to think when seeking sex by internet. If you *must* think, don't let on.

Thought is bad enough, but the incapacity to keep such thought out of conversation is a real vaginal adversary. So, even if I *could* have found sex—and the chap from the next suburb who went by the name hard_4_ewe would have uncritically provided it that night, and probably often in the future if I had dressed, as he requested, in wool, to which I am mildly allergic—I did a marvellous job of talking my way out of it.

I could not do sexy chat that night any more than I could visit Tuscany. I was terrible at this business. And rude and terribly impatient.

I have retained copies of some of the messages exchanged in the hours after the ex left. They are embarrassing to read and may as well be a reverse playbook in How to Get Laid in a Hurry. I reproduce a selection of these for the purposes of instruction. Horny just-dumped persons who cannot afford a ticket to Italy: that which follows is how *not* to find sex by app.

I had promoted my genitals that night to both men and women. Nonetheless, correspondents were exclusively male and many of these, noting my 'bisexual' category, asked, 'Are you a Lesbian?' or, more commonly, 'r u Lesbian?'

For me, internet abbreviations and poor spelling were unsexy problems. If you are similarly troubled, you will likely remain so. Don't bother trying to repair your irreparable aversion. But there is another habit you and I might do well to break when we find ourselves in sex chat. Argue about apostrophes by all means, but do not argue with people over fine points of morality, such as international relations, or, say, the offside rule. Or, as in my case, queer politics.

What you should not do, for example, when somebody asks you 'Are you a Lesbian?' is answer:

MuffDiva: No. And why are you capitalising 'Lesbian'? In the course of our communications, you have shunned capital letters where they are needed—and don't even get me started on your other style crimes that start but hardly end in a confusion of 'your' with 'you're' or 'ur'.

But a word that does not demand capitalisation is the one to which it is perversely applied. Where is the capital H for Helen? The capital M for Melbourne? Nowhere. And yet you enlist their close neighbour 'L' for 'Lesbian'. If you can't observe the basic rules of usage, then I can't see how you could find my muff with both hands and Google Maps.

I took a screenshot of that answer to the question 'Are you a Lesbian?' and sent it to Celine for assessment. She replied, 'Total boner-killer, you fucking idiot, Razer.' As, I imagine, is:

> **MuffDiva:** No. It is true that I am female and it is true that I was, until this afternoon, in a relationship with a female with whom I had sex of diminishing quality and frequency over a period of fifteen years. But, no. I am not now nor have I ever been a member of the Lesbian Party. Rather than join that union, I'd eat devilled ham every day for a month. I am not fond of manufactured meat and I am even less fond of the query, 'Are you a Lesbian?' Do not ask again. This sort of questioning diminishes us both and I will have none of your venereal McCarthyism.

Just don't do this. Confess to being a capital L Lesbian without correcting usage. Prefer simple speech over extravagant style. And please do not mention Senator Joseph McCarthy and the House Un-American Activities Committee, except in the unusual case you are talking to a horny history buff with a particular interest in dissident-themed sex games. Who is possibly Mr Dean. Send him my best.

*

Although I am attempting, wherever possible, to universalise my experience for the sake of the broader dumped population, I should admit that my sensitivity to the whole 'Lesbian' issue is *probably* pretty specific to me. Please forgive this indulgence. (And all those many to follow.)

That my particular desertion happened to be of a homosexual flavour intensified my shame and my impatience with views on sexuality generally. 'Lesbians' are really not supposed to break up, these days. They are supposed to stay together forever and provide an inspiring liberal example to others. And, this, notwithstanding my actual intention to stay together forever, was an attitude that really ticked me off.

Regularly washing the socks, or licking the vagina of another woman are largely seen as acts of moral leadership in the West. If there is one thing now more socially shameful than being part of a homosexual relationship, it is being expelled from a homosexual relationship. Almost no one, save for parents and preachers, hopes for the end of a homosexual relationship any more.

So many people expect us to be so damn good, as evidenced when I changed my Facebook relationship status to 'Single'— I did wait an entire half hour following the ex's departure to do this—and someone messaged me to say, 'That is a shame! You two were so inspiring.' (I un-friended them, and so did Celine at my request.)

I have never been comfortable with or tolerant of the belief that anyone, especially me, can serve to genuinely inspire others. Like my history teacher Mr Dean, I do not think that good or bad things spring from good or bad people. I believe they are produced by the mechanism of history.

And I believe that, historically, it's an awful time to be a homosexual.

At some point, gay became the new beige and we are today the class doomed to revive the discarded dream of marriage. We are the people charged with conspicuous carriage of rainbow babies in expensive baby slings. Ours are the animal libidos that must now be concealed behind a whopping great flag that reads 'family' and 'love'. We can no longer really cry for any rights, other than those that would see us domesticated and neutered and compelled to give our desire a single name. Or possibly sent to the army.

Anyhow. People like to see us freaks in pairs. This has always got on my tits but, for obvious reasons, never quite so much as it did that first night.

*

This 'lesbian' thing makes plain another problem internet sex ladies face. This problem, however, has a solution. Girls, whether you're Divorce Horn honkers or more wholesomely engorged, pretend that you are *not* interested in penises. Even if you are directly asked 'Are you a horny bitch?', answer NO. (Unless, of course, you are talking with hard_4_ewe, who really doesn't mind either way. Just so long as you have agreed to dress as livestock.) My advice to all women speaking with internet sex men is: in general, appear unmotivated, a bit stupid and very hard-to-get.

Challenges are sought by most men on XXX dating apps. Which is peculiar if one bothers to think about it. Within these apps we are required to geolocate our genitals and check a series of boxes indicating tolerance of things like 'anal', 'edgeplay' and 'adult nursing'. In this, any pretence of challenge is a great hypocrisy. I mean, we're obviously up for it and, in many cases, eager to accessorise it, vandalise it and slather it in baby lotion.

Still. Indifference is a great internet sex tactic for ladies. Take an attitude of 'Yeah, whatever' for some time before revealing only very mild arousal, which should never approach the 'horny bitch' level explicitly demanded but implicitly rejected by many men of the internet.

I would suggest that the words usually appended to internet pictures advertising fictional Russian sluts are a good style guide. See, 'Hi. I'm Natasha and I'm so bored.' Act as if you made a wrong turn on the internet. You fell into a XXX app by mistake while actually looking for a gingham pinafore to wear on Sundays. You're a naïf with no interest in penises at all and, oops-a-daisy, how did my tiny little church dress come off while I was making a chain of paper dolls and strolling through this meadow grass? Oh, Mister Man, please don't break me, etc., etc.

The innocent unconcern of women is best in most heterosexual cases, save for those that follow the cougar convention—just a simple reversal in which the younger man must pretend to be reluctant and the older woman must pretend to be predatory. This, of course, is another compromise to libido. But it was one I was prepared to make if it meant a chance at meeting the user Datagasm. 'Nice pic,' as they say on the internet.

Late that night, I chatted with the young man happily until he described himself to me as 'cougar pray'. His picture depicted a handsome, nerdish sort and, being partial to a hottie with hints of a neurodevelopmental disorder, I might have overlooked this spelling error had he not repeated it.

Datagasm: Let me be your pray.

Which annoyed me, not just because it was such an awful misspelling, but because I felt about as physically forceful as poached lettuce that night. The thought of preying on anyone, even a young C++ coder who looked quite a bit like Nikola Tesla, was exhausting.

'That's a homophone mistake,' I wrote.

He replied, 'But I am fine with gay people.'

I became critically weary of such errors by sun-up. And not just because I am a vile cow with unrealised literary pretensions, but because errors of typing and understanding made masturbation very difficult.

A sex chat full of mistakes is as distracting as a pornographic video whose stars are wearing Christmas antlers; or, for the posher reader, a ballet whose principal dancer can't stop passing gas.

An early-riser wrote to me, 'I want to pond your as.' At first I thought this chap might be writing poetry in some new transcendentalist style, but as I came to realise that he wanted to 'pound' my 'arse', I began to misplace all my hopes and dreams. This was not *Walden*.

To be clear, I have no particular interest in defending Thoreau, in whose verse I am no expert, and none in maligning sodomy whatsoever. I am an inexpert fan of sodomy. But sodomy is a reasonably delicate act and, in my view, demands to be spelled correctly. So I told Henry David this arse pounding could only be arranged with notice for those days when my haemorrhoids were not acting up.

When he said that I was 'disgusting', I pasted some notes on colorectal surgery into the dating app. Et, tu, Brute? I wasn't the one who demanded misspelled anal. But, this is really my problem, not his, and probably not yours. However, I will say that you should probably turn off notifications for your XXX app for several hours *even* on your most sex-starved day because you too, whether male or female, may find yourself talking about proctology from sheer frustration. Or, doing even dumber stuff, such as that which follows.

THE HELEN 100

By seven in the morning, a man sent me my first dick pic. This may seem shocking to those over thirty and/or unfamiliar with adult online dating, but it is a customary trade, particularly when offered to a woman who posted a picture of her tits. How a lady should respond here is, 'Oo, gee, that's a nice big one. I hope it doesn't break me,' and perhaps provide a picture of her muff. You do not do as I did.

Very Serious and Quite Long Public Service Announcement for Horny Bitches, Bucks and Those of Liquid Gender Looking For Sex on the Internet: Any person of any sort considering publication of a urogenital self-portrait must remember to edit. Your pink bits should be displayed in the strictest isolation from distinguishing features such as face, tattoo or greaseproof chicken bag. Your identifying data should be digitally removed. And I know this sounds difficult, but there's an app for that and for fuck's sake, look it up if you don't want hard_4_ewe learning your address and popping over with a pair of rusted shears. Life, especially the post-dumped one, is difficult enough without courting impatient perverts and/or future revenge porn, so let's learn to use a little thrift in the dirty-picture-sharing economy, shall we? I cannot believe how much data people leak online. A *street address* might very well be embedded on that picture of your thing. If an irresponsible tool like me can remember to remove all identifying information from a crotch-shot, then you can, too. Sure, I may have since had unprotected sex with several unwholesome persons, and at least one who quite urgently needed a bath. But I never once accidentally published my GPS coordinates. True, this was due less to caution, of which at the time I had none, than it was to a habit derived from workplace familiarity with graphics software—due to their habit of copyright theft, the Daily Deals people had been as serious about file data purging as they were about the need for fun. Anyhow. Whatever your profession, you must wear a digital prophylactic.

I didn't respond with a picture of my muff because I had now completely lost my lolly. Instead I Photoshopped the image of his penis onto the forehead of a cartoon unicorn in place of its mythical horn, and set this as my profile picture.

I was mean and tired and apparently determined to spurn sex, however much I wanted it.

Obviously, this lack of immediate sex was chiefly my doing. My arrogance and my broken capacity for fantasy—I could never dare to dream—were largely at fault. But it wasn't *all* my fault. The repertoire of online hetero-sexy-talk is extraordinarily limited and would drive many fair-minded persons to rudeness. And, finally, to sleep with Eleven on the floor.

4

Eighteen hours and one terabyte of shame since she left

'You are restricting my right to freely communicate,' she said.

'I must not be subject to exile,' she said.

The phone had tipped me from a shallow morning of sleep and into a now familiar lecture. This was the way she had come to speak to me when incensed: like the International Charter for Human Rights. When she was angry, she was also very official.

A few months back, I recalled, she'd been cross with my careless tidying of her collage materials from the dinner table. 'You need to understand that this is a violation,' she had said. 'We all have the right to creative expression.'

Now this may well be a general truth, but, in this case, elevated a trivial domestic mistake to a global war crime. It had also, in my view then, overlooked my own 'right' to creative expression, which was violated daily by the work of writing discount beauty coupons. After all, I had grumbled only to myself, their tiresome production funded all those unprofitable afternoons of collage.

When I'd been censured so officially for moving old magazines to make way for the night's meal, I had very much wanted to say, 'Oh, fuck off, Bono. Go and write a song about your pain,' but refrained. Especially as she had just prepared the German Dish, which always hit the spot on even the coldest days we spent together.

But I did say it now, over the phone, and this set her off on a very long Nuremberg statement full of 'freedom' and 'inalienable' and 'abnegation of my right to freely and creatively correspond'.

You see, before I'd gone to sleep with Eleven on the chicken that previous night, I'd thought to call the phone company and asked them to bar her calls to international or 1900 numbers.

Certainly this was mean of me, but it wasn't totally Reich Ministry. I did it in part, of course, because I was a spiteful dumped person whose chief pleasure had quickly become the creation of inconvenience for the absconded. But I did it mostly because the phone was billed to me. If she had used the phone to make a five-hundred-dollar international or 1900 call, I, a now un-waged person, would soon have been flat broke.

I hadn't supposed that she did harbour any particular plans to make a five-hundred-dollar international or 1900 call.

However, I now knew firsthand that emotionally exhausted persons could be rash with their mobile devices. They may find themselves Skyping a shamanic psychic in Reykjavik (I really can't bear to talk about it and so omit this moment of expensive spiritualism from my account; but I will say that I have found no use in knowing the identity of my spirit animal) or, perhaps, publishing pictures of penis-unicorns—uniporns?—on the internet at 7 a.m. So I barred the phone (and, okay, lowered the credit card limit), but not entirely out of kneejerk fascism. I did it chiefly to safeguard against expensive mistakes which, following my fun farewell note to Brynlee, I knew I could no longer afford to correct.

As she continued with the rousing 'rights' speech in which I was cast as Goebbels—'This is an assault not only against my freedom but my *safety*'—it occurred to me that she *had* tried to make a five-hundred-dollar international or 1900 call and was now Security Council-level angry that she'd failed. She was much angrier than I had heard in some time. She was so angry she even eventually forgot to be tedious. She left the United Nations altogether and became a rogue state. 'YOU ARE A DEVIL HEGEMON! DEATH TO YOU! I WILL WIPE YOU OFF THE MAP' style of thing.

'You have always been such a fucking controlling bitch,' is what I believe she said.

Excluding the possibility of her absolute batshit madness, I deduced just two explanations for the force of her rage. The first and most probable was that she'd developed an internet crush on some poetry trollop from Shittington Falls, Vermont, or wherever, and found herself without wi-fi and in urgent want of a dirty international phone call. The second was that she had an emotional need to be angry with me and had selected this handy cause after failing to find a truly notable one. Which, to be honest, seemed pretty unlikely as I had long provided quite notable cause.

It's not as though I had done a single terrible thing as a spouse. I had, however, *been* a pretty terrible thing. She had lived with my tiresome depression, my tiresome anxiety and my tiresome face, which had done a particularly poor job of concealing its distaste for her, most television news commentators and everything that wasn't Eleven the cat for months. Possibly even a year or two.

So if she felt like making me responsible for the end of our relationship, she could have easily done it.

She could have mentioned my undisciplined weeping or farting or the many months writing discount beauty coupons in elasticised pants shrieking 'I am so much better than this! I could be writing trenchant analysis for *The Times*! Prize-winning literary nonfiction! Fucking, I don't know, acrostic poems!' I was not a model of quiet selflessness; my sacrifice had long been, like my flatulence, fairly audible.

She, on the other hand, had always been rather good at concealing her rage. She rarely tried to gain loudly what could be more fully won by measured speech. She knew as all the modern world's most effective parents and leaders do: the best way to strip someone of their will is to delude them into thinking they retain it.

The brutal father who beats his son for failing to excel in football is likely to be disappointed. The liberal father who *convinces* his son that excellence in football was the kid's own idea sees results. The boss who tells her workers they are worthless will not easily extract extra profit from their bodies. The boss who tells her workers they are 'empowered' to work unpaid overtime will succeed. This work is fun! FUN!

'If you want a vision of the future, imagine a boot stamping on a human face.' *Nah*. If you really want a vision of the future, don't listen to old George Orwell. Instead consider the possibility that, one day, you'll be buying your own fashionable boot from a Daily Deals email and stamping your own damn face with it. Just as I had been for several of these fifteen years.

Real power learns to hide itself behind stylish boots and moderate phrases—a war is a 'dispute', a firing is a 'negotiated departure' and a relationship breakdown is an 'uncoupling' or, worse, an 'opportunity to grow'.

Orwell wasn't right about the character of the boot, but he was certainly right about the mild language that would emerge to underplay its force.

I was completely habituated to polite fascist newspeak at home, even if it had long since begun to give me the shits at work. The ex had always known how to impose her will through the appearance of quiet reason and, as conscious as I had become of this tactic, I was by no means immune to its power. Her expensively educated, reasonable voice would bend me to its domestic will every time. That voice always set the tone and terms for our life. It had led us to a particular suburb, me to particular work and miseries. I did as I was told by that voice. So long as I permitted myself to believe I had volition, I would do exactly as it uttered.

I *wanted* to write sales tripe and forgo creative indulgence. I *longed* to live miles from the nearest tram. *Honestly*, I *adored* a life spent in tears, elastic and resentment.

All these blows were struck by me—and, to be honest, even relished by me so long as I was loved. But, even though I had inflicted them, they had always been prompted by her expensive, reasonable voice.

'I would like us to move together graciously towards a shift in our intimacy and in view of that, I ask that you redeem my access to international and 1900 calls' is exactly the sort of expensive thing I might have predicted she'd have said. And the sort of thing I'd heed. Not something just a little short of, 'Fuck you, devil. I want you to pay for all my international phone sex.'

Well. What she actually said was, 'You have always controlled our fucking finances. You are a fascist.'

While it was certainly true that I had always controlled our finances, it was not at all true that I fascistically relished this chore. This 'control' had been imposed by and certainly not wrested from someone who showed any interest in regulating the movement of money. She and I had been, in fact, given to joke about her unconcern for cash and sometimes hypothesised warmly that she suffered a form of fiscal dyslexia. 'Did you earn a bajillion dollars today?' she might say, and we'd laugh.

Like a lot of people who went to nice schools, she just never learned how to understand value. Sometimes, she would be shocked by the price of baked beans and sometimes, she would think little before approving the cost of a business class airfare. Two dollars could be outrageous and four thousand could be a bargain.

For years, I had admired her freedom from value. More lately, I had begun to see it as the product of her freedom from labour and my slavery to a wage. She created whatever she fancied for fun; I made terrible things for money. I had started to offer her short reports on value when she spent. And she *spent*. 'That's four days' of my labour,' I said before she sent out nine of her unprofitable artworks for quality framing. 'I have the right to creative expression,' she said in her very best envoy's voice when I received the Visa statement.

Her rightful creative expression was very expensively framed.

That expensive voice almost always worked. Even now it would have swayed me to reverse the phone bar. It would have prompted me to pack her things into boxes, agree that this entire break-up was for the best and ask if she would like some help selecting a new Indonesian throw rug that might accommodate the global tastes of her glitter-feral whore from Shittington Falls.

If the ex had remonstrated with me reasonably, told me my company had lately been about as vital and productive as a conference call with Brynlee, I would have listened. I would have complied. I would have restored the Visa to its previous unmanageable limit. I would not have become immediately suspicious and we'd have parted in proper UN style.

But her diplomacy had failed her, and I saw a rare opportunity for control. I said, 'Restraint could serve us better now than a tantrum,' which made me sound if less than a diplomat, then at least like a reputable headmistress. I thought a headmistress might mollify a private schoolgirl.

But she responded like a rebel teen who believes with every ascending decibel that she distances herself from guilt. She reached a falsely virtuous crescendo and screamed, 'I have my rights to speech! This is unconscionable! Jihad against Helen! Devil Helen must die!' or similar.

I was now certain that she had fallen in with some free-verse glow-stick harlot with turquoise hair and a clit ring. I *knew* it. I knew her uncharacteristic fit was borne of shame or guilt. And possibly a bit of punishing horniness, which, as I had lately discovered, can tend to send one mad.

She was almost certainly cheating on me, I realised.

In fact, now I think about it, she'd adhered to a fairly textbook execution of The Ten Signs He's Cheating That Women Ignore. What follows is an incomplete account of these Signs—I'm very emotional recounting the ignominy, so you can't expect me to remember all ten.

In recent months, she had taken a keen and unprecedented interest in both **physical fitness** and **grooming**. She had even asked for advance details of the dozen discount beauty deals I uploaded each day. She had *got herself dolphined*.

There had been **unexplained** or poorly explained **absences**.

There had been **great shifts of affection**. There were morning hymns to my excellence followed by afternoons that keened for the death of my goodness. She hated me or she feted me in the few minutes a day that we actually met.

She spent the rest of her time affixed to **social media** and she always, always jumped when her **phone** sounded an alert.

Once or twice very **late at night,** I had awoken to see her creep into her shed where she kept her computer. She was wearing maximum make-up and minimum lingerie. I had asked her what she was doing and she had told me to go back to sleep. 'Just trying out a new look for you,' she said.

She was almost certainly cheating on me. Which I would have known if only I had more regularly read women's lifestyle publications.

She was cheating on me.

Good, I thought, which is not to say that I longed for her faithlessness. Being a wronged wife had never been a fetish and I didn't expect to take pleasure in the role right now. But I knew being cuckolded could provide me if not with an orgasm then (a) a traditional set of behavioural guidelines in a chaotic time and (b) relief from the boredom of my just-dumped self.

I was not consumed with jealousy. Instead I was hopeful that I would soon have something to truly whine about, some solid indignity into which to sink my rotten old fangs. I was grateful for the possibility of a real boot in the face.

I did not wish particularly to know beyond doubt that she had failed me. But I did want a pause from the thoughts of my own dreary failings. I looked forward to humming a few verses of 'Your Cheatin' Heart' as I imagined this could provide a nice break from hours of emotional self-harm, chicken and Photoshopping with phalluses. I could now loathe her and her infidelity, instead of myself and the bleak and shitty habits into which I'd certainly fallen.

I mentioned none of my suspicions by telephone and I hung up after wishing her a 'pigfucking day', one of many cathartic phrases Celine had texted me for use during initial post-break-up contact.

I picked up the dear cat, whom I encouraged to shit on the collage materials in a shed that would soon be as full of damning proof as it was of bad incense and art. Eleven had just begun to scratch a pile of doll hair when I found much of the fuel I'd need for a very righteous fire. It took me no time at all to find two carefully preserved notes handwritten by a woman, who I had met a few times, named Sandra. Arty fucking Sandra.

The first note contained a jejune reference to Greek mythology, something or other about them being muses and artists, and how they were both each other's inspiration and each other's sculptor, or some shit. The second mentioned the 'erotic charge' of 'total collaboration' that had, apparently, taken place in this very shed.

Sandra had enclosed a tasteful selfie of her tits, which was monochrome and, it irked me to concede, much more carefully composed than my own tit pic of the previous evening. It was a pretty good photo, really, and I should have kept it as a visual reference to attract tasteful suitors instead of wiping my stinking armpits on it and throwing it at a homemade candle in the ex's collection.

I had not come to know this Sandra person very well in the few months she had been popping by to 'collaborate' with the ex. This was partly because she was one of those annoying arty fuckers who always referred to rooms as 'spaces'; exactly the sort I successfully avoid—well, everywhere except inside my most intimate relationship. It was chiefly because I strongly suspected her of wanting to lez out with my wife.

I had voiced these concerns several times to the ex, but been assured that the collaboration was strictly creative. She had even cried and said to me in the kitchen she was *outraged* I could *think* such a thing! Sandra is married and straight, don't you know? Why did I have to *sexualise* everything? This was about *art*.

Well, unless the exchange of hand jobs in a backyard shed is what passes as an extended performance piece these days—and it possibly is—they hadn't been making art. According to the note, they'd been going at some pretty standard lez adultery while I was metres away.

'Helen was working just metres away when you first touched my most familiar part,' wrote Arty Sandra. Yes, I *fucking was*. Metres away writing discount coupons. Discount fucking coupons for fucking frizz ensmoothenation.

I was still not truly annoyed about the infidelity itself, but I *was* annoyed to learn that they had *acknowledged* I paid for the act with my cheerless labour. I became *outraged* to think that my labour had functioned as something of a stimulant. They were at it hammer and tongs in part *because* I was toiling in misery.

Helen was working just metres away.

*

How did my working week come to operate as atmospheric; as some sort of inspiring sex doll? My labour had made their leisure not only more possible, but more *pleasurable. This* disgrace was the one that I chose as my boot.

Once, I read an interview with a famous sociologist who wanted to make the point that communists were far too fanatical in ascribing all human difficulty to the conditions of labour. Why, he wanted to know, do they always make everything about money? He said something like, 'Not every problem someone has with their girlfriend is due to the capitalist mode of production.' Well, this girlfriend problem *was,* you silly sociology man. As I saw it, my labour had become her aphrodisiac and so, I became angrier than even the angriest trade unionist.

I called Sandra at the art 'space' in which I knew she worked. I asked to speak with the home-wrecking scab in charge. I belted out my domestic version of the 'Internationale'. I would not stand for this worker's violation.

I can't be certain what I actually said to Arty Sandra, but I may have unfavourably mentioned her harem pants and/or fondness for the music of Amanda Palmer. I may have said something about her exchange of white liberal guilt for dangly fair-trade earrings made by foreign women who would be forever in servitude to Western micro-loans. I may have told her that her vag smelled of marinated tofu past its Best Before date, and not of the spotless pages of the Patricia Highsmith novel, which I was pretty certain she had immediately purchased following her first midlife lez-out, which had taken place in *my* fucking shed with the body of *my* fucking spouse. Ex-spouse. You scab.

Whatever I said, it sounded at least as half as unpleasant to me as the music of Amanda Palmer as soon as I had finished saying it. Perhaps being Wronged was not a very good fit for me.

Sandra's two young children had names whose fashionable spelling put each of them at risk of a literacy disorder. There was no honour at all in mentioning this, but I am pretty sure I did. I felt awful poking fun at Junyper and Stellan and immediately regretted my threats to fill their biodynamic juice bottles with high fructose corn syrup at their Montessori school. Or telling her that I would secretly vaccinate both of them the next time she was at her Kundalini class. Or that I would creep into her kitchen and mix the heirloom seeds she sprouted for this indigo pair with some GMO Monsanto stock.

I felt quite rotten about abusing Sandra and her arty family.

As nutty and narcissistic as I had become by that second day, I understood that Sandra had probably been as deluded about the rules of the shed as me. In all likelihood, we'd both heard many falsehoods.

I knew that the ex's lack of scruples in her dealings with me by no means indicated an oversupply of them to Sandra. Who knows what she had told Arty Sandra to tempt her into congress. That we had an 'open relationship'? That things had been 'bad for a while'?

If the correspondence was any guide, she had certainly told Arty Sandra that she was a working artist, which is a generous way to depict a life spent largely at the mouth of a beer bottle while waving a pair of scissors about and posting animal videos to Facebook.

Having concluded this fairly shameful phone call with some crack about shoving a Jasper Johns assemblage down her awful cheesecloth top, I found in the bin a third and fourth note penned by Sandra. These had not been pressed into a scrapbook as the others were but were discarded, presumably due to their contents, which advised discontinuation of the shed-sex. Sandra didn't want it anymore.

Perhaps guilt had overcome desire. Perhaps Sandra hadn't really taken to lezzing out—quite possible, as I faintly recall her saying to me 'I didn't even lick her vagina'. I wondered if she'd seen the vagina pre- or post-tarantula. I wondered if she knew that vagina had felt the pain of beauty biocide for the first time for her—a vaginal waxing into which *my* Eleni had been unwittingly drawn. I wondered if Sandra had come to suspect that my ex really wasn't much of a committed artist. I'm not sure of the reason and I don't know if Sandra was either, as she had failed to explain it over two quite long Dear John letters.

I called for another chicken and decided to apologise to Sandra. I had said some very cruel things about the woman's wardrobe that I believed demanded reparation. It probably wasn't her fault that she dressed like the manager of a vegan food truck—at any rate, I think such costume was compulsory in her suburb.

The apology to Sandra, I told myself, was for *immediate action*. It had to be made *now* and finished in time for chicken. NOW. Now.

This keen concern for the feelings of someone who had, after all, rogered my spouse in the shed while I was writing discount coupons seems odd to me in the present. I think it would seem odd to many persons. A free verbal hit at the wispy progressive who screwed your spouse during business hours would, I think, be generally excused by most.

I should have permitted myself this most permissible lapse, which, I think, even Arty Sandra had felt that she deserved—she had cried and said two or three times, 'I am sorry, but I was just so very lonely. My husband left. I am sorry. I *was* sorry.' I should have ignored the drive to atone. But, at the time, redress felt urgent. As urgent as the need to be rogered or to cry or to quit my job had the night before. *NOW. Now. I must act now.*

I imagine many dumped people are trodden by this parade of emotional purpose. We are marched by emotion from one ostensibly vital mission to the next. We find it impossible to stop. We convince ourselves we need sex, we need retribution, we need forgiveness THIS MINUTE, when what we actually need *this minute* is a nice bath and a rest.

Public Service Announcement: Have a bath.

When I was a teenager, I used to laugh at my grandmother, Grace, who thought that there was little that could not be cured with a sleep, a bath or an early dinner. She thought that organisation and a little care were all that it took for a life to be good. I used to tease her about this advice and insist that life, of which I'd then had no experience, was *so* much more complicated, and that she just *didn't understand* big problems.

But, of course, she really did. She lived through the two wars, the Great Depression and an emotionally violent marriage.

It has taken me decades of more everyday conflict to see that a nice bath *can* make life easier. It doesn't fix everything, but it can fix a fuck of a lot.

If you have recently been called to war or given your spousal marching orders, do try at some point to have a nice bath. Also, try disabling all communications devices and/or swallowing the keys to your house and your car. Try anything to slow the procession of impulses. Particularly those that are vengeful, which are almost always best left until they shrivel. And, I'm telling you, they always will.

This is not to say that I did not indulge revenge fantasy, or that I acted in a smooth and Christian manner. Or that I do not now remain somewhat shitty that I had been so intimately deceived. Or that I did not watch women's divorce films on Netflix. Those whose first act sees some sassy lady set fire, for example, to her cheating husband's Aston Martin.

Oh, I watched them.

'You go, girl,' I probably said to the screen, and hummed along to the inevitable Aretha whose anthem of feminine selfhood heralded an hour of affecting ups-and-downs. Whoa! Respect!

I relished the scenes that moved towards the completion of a heroine, who grows wiser and more beautiful and whose newfound blaze of independence, first sparked by arson, eventually brings her the most fulfilling kind of fire with Bradley Cooper, or whoever.

I can't be expected to recall the details of any film I watched back then. But I do remember that the newly dumped lady *really* needs a bath and a rest.

I do not mean you should not act like a nut-loaf or even that you must forgive. I do, however, ask you to understand that real break-ups contain very few plot points, opportunities for growth or handsome men. Life contains little that films or revenge fantasies do and a good deal that they do not. As life contains things such as insurance, family law and fire safety standards, you're really best to stay away from camera-friendly fire.

Pyromania won't seem like a good idea in five minutes, so please, if you are considering the destruction of a luxury sports car, or similar, get in the bath or have a short walk and take the time to calm the flip down.

In the silence, you will recognise the likelihood that you will be arrested. You will come to know that the personal growth and independence experienced by ladies in films do not always generate a Bradley Cooper. And, if your household does boast an Aston Martin, you will remember that you are sufficiently wealthy to retain the kind of solicitor who can probably negotiate the lawful immolation of that car. Take a minute. Get a lawyer. Outsource all destruction.

Invaluable time- and cost-saving realisations of the type aforementioned can only unfold when you take a minute. Please, take a minute.

*

As I had happened to hurl my phone into a heap of possum bones—which had begun to smell, as many of her 'found objects' did, of gingivitis and old clothes—I had a minute to take. I would not call Sandra as I had been planning—after all, there was a very good chance I'd lose my lolly again and tell her to go fuck herself with a farm gate loaf of ancient grains. As it was presently too difficult to reach my phone, which was still lying in art's graveyard, I thought for a minute and decided that I would write Arty Sandra a letter if not of apology, then one of sober explanation.

I sat down at the ex's PC to compose a *De Profundis* and Eleven the cat looked at me and said, 'I give you about fifteen seconds before you give up on that and go and hack her Facebook.'

He was right.

Yes, I know. This is not a very defensible act. I am myself strongly opposed to data surveillance, and once I even sent Edward Snowden's people a donation. However, I am prepared to bet that even the most ardent privacy activist is wont to dig when she starts reading a story about herself.

I should never have started, of course, but once I did, it was very difficult to stop. I partook of the Helen is an Unfeeling Cow narrative for an hour or two. It was a real page-turner.

I first found a months-long message chain with a vile writer friend of hers in which she had described me as a 'necessary bank account' and, more lately, Sandra as 'a clit tease'.

I never liked this guy. He had too much money, far too many recovered memories, and once at dinner had told my ex to follow his example and not to bother reading books by any of the great philosophers. Which was, in my view, a bit like one bad dog telling another not to bother pissing outdoors. She hardly needed the discouragement.

'Helen is totally a controlling total night mare who you should leave,' wrote the vile writer, giving weight to my long-standing doubt that his popular memoirs were not substantially improved by an editor.

I did totally feel a bit like a total, controlling nightmare. With every deceit of hers that I discovered, I became more deceitful.

It is deceitful to snoop, even on a deceiver. *But* it's also tremendously cathartic—especially if it turns out that there's something to find. Personally, I found myself progressing through grief at a very good clip and I can't say that I wouldn't recommend the practice to those of you blessed with a dodgy ex who has neglected to change any of their passwords. I'll leave you to work out the ethics of ends versus means out on your own.

Things were moving very fast. Another chicken had arrived.

'Here's a tasty chook for a tasty lady!' lied the chicken man again. I gave Eleven the better part of a breast and retained a wing for myself. It was the first morsel in twenty-four hours for which my stomach had a chamber and, as I ate, sugars briefly reignited my search-rage.

I read and comprehended the details of her deceit quickly. I also became bored quickly. After all, there's only so much arty midlife adultery the average reader can take.

Having read three accounts of a first kiss with Sandra outside Junyper's archery class, and a few more of a first tiff endured on the drive home from a farmers' market, where they'd resolved their differences over a terrine made of humanely raised duck, I found it was pretty dull reading. And not just because accounts of affairs, especially those between conspicuously liberal, arty fuckers who press flowers and letters and seek to ban the use of trans fats from local eating establishments, are dull to everyone but the participants.

I stopped reading not only because this love, or whatever they had, followed a fairly standard course but because I came to see that nothing, not even surveillance, could ever really upturn an answer to a complicated question like loss. I could spend hours gathering intelligence, but I saw that I would learn nothing of real emotional value.

It struck me then that no one can really elaborate on 'It's over.' It's just over. And it doesn't matter why. Here, the history of disaster is not at all useful. History, as Mr Dean had taught me, is invaluable in understanding war. But it's of little utility in understanding love. *Not every problem you have with your girlfriend*, etc.

She broke my heart by leaving me that evening. Then, she broke it again the next day by betrayal. This wasn't fate, nor was it determined by the movements of history or of capital. It didn't have to be this way—as the shopping list for our next week of dinners still stuck on the fridge continued to remind me. She'd been making plans for *us*, even if she had also been making plans for herself. She still loved us a little, until yesterday. It didn't have to be this way, but this was the way that it was.

5

Twenty-four hours, one infidelity and one therapy appointment since she left
This Way of Zen attitude I took to the whole shemozzle didn't last very long. I was all go-with-the-flow for, maybe, seven seconds, and then, just before an hour of suicidal ideation so unpleasant I would call upon Cheap Gerard, I began to take pictures of my vagina.

This started when a man on the XXX app, to which I'd been attached since download, asked me, 'Do you love pussy?' Of course, this is a great improvement on 'r u Lesbian?', but one that hit me in the wrong instant.

Did I love pussy? I wasn't sure at all if this remained the case. Perhaps I now feared it.

Once, before I met Eleven, a shelter tabby of undocumented charm, I visited a sale of Scottish Fold cats with the intention to purchase. I saw a queen in heat. Her vulva was enormous, terrifying and a little bit comic. It looked as if a cheap props department on a Z-grade monster movie had taken a deflated inner tube from a bicycle, twisted it into a pretzel and spray-painted it pink in readiness for attack by a plastic sword.

The queen backed her vulva-prop into everything, including me, her litter box, and the wall, yowling a sex-starved lament. Fuck me. Fuck ME. FUCK ME. This, I think, is pretty much how I would have seemed that day to any human—which was most every human, including the barbecue chicken man—who provoked my desire. A huge pink reeking hole so comically needy, it goaded only laughter and fear.

As I am certain you will understand, checking my own hole for evidence of fangs etc. was necessary at this point. And so, I took several pictures for personal use.

A photograph may seem silly to you, but it was practical in my case as I am legally blind. I had tried investigation by hand mirror and found that it revealed little; just something that looked like a nimbus of fairy floss with fresh bite marks in it. It was a family-friendly anime vagina. I knew my dolphin couldn't be that delightful, so I took a digital picture and zoomed in.

The clear view of my organ troubled me no more than the cloudy one. I was not shocked. I have not been shocked for many years by the HD lens of late pornography, which takes, as you may know, a very anatomical view of muff.

I was never truly shocked by her vagina. I was not shocked by my vagina, and many of the other real-life and represented vaginas I have seen in the past were not at all troubling. But I suppose this is because I had always worked up to the anxiety of vaginas slowly, including the one I looked at now.

One does not simply enter a vagina. We prepare with a brief prayer to ourselves. We transform the horror of this otherwise banished thing into a source of good. It's a bit like Communion in reverse.

Like the chaps I met on the internet, even those who claim to adore 'horny bitches' but in fact fear them, I found bold female desire, in this case my own, to be quite monstrous. Not just by me, I decided, but by everyone. I shared these thoughts as soon as I had them with persons of the XXX community.

After a fairly good look at my dolphin, to I_Heart_Pussy, I replied,

MuffDiva: Do I love pussy? Well, both absolutely yes and absolutely no. I desire it, yet I loathe it. But isn't this true of all desired things? I have come in recent minutes to believe that desire is intrinsically repulsive, even the apparently gingham sort experienced by Renée Zellweger in the film *Jerry Maguire*. 'You complete me' is a horrifying thing to say, if you think about it. You complete me. You fill my bloody void.

I_Heart_Pussy: lol, wut?

MuffDiva: Perhaps in order to feel the damage of pleasure, we must all be prepared to be broken. That we all must break ourselves. What do you think?

I_Heart_Pussy: Are you into bondage?

MuffDiva: Well, probably, but that's not my point. My point is, I think all people are probably all as horrible as me. Even the nice ones. Don't you agree? I am lying on the floor with my hair full of chicken and my hands down my pants, and I think about those well-dressed divorced ladies who are feeling what I'm feeling and how they go to Tuscany on tours. Imagine them sitting in a luxury coach trying not to think about golden showers or of slicing off a priest's todger and ramming it down the several throats of pigeons in an ancient public square while shrieking, 'Eat daddy, dirty bird.' Perhaps as they brought themselves to violent anal climax with a votive.

I_Heart_Pussy: Right. So you're just divorced. I know what that's like, mate. I've been there.

It wasn't the intention of I_Heart_Pussy to break me with these words, but he did.

Public Service Announcement: Psychologists, even quite bad ones, are valuable to the newly dumped.

Perhaps owing to his tendency of popping out midway through a consultation to smoke, Cheap Gerard was very cheap. But he had a reasonable reputation; particularly for smoking cessation. When I asked him during the emergency post-dump session that second day, 'How do I live now?', I was pretty sure he'd have a good solution.

First, he asked me to sign something called a 'no-harm agreement'. This basically meant that I promised not to top myself and he promised to talk to me, should I feel it were needed, in person, any time. In a smoking environment, obviously.

Then he talked about the separation as an 'opportunity for growth'. Naturally, I told him to get fucked. He toyed with his cigarette lighter. Then I asked him what 'growth', of which I'd recently heard so fucking much, meant and how it might be achieved. He spoke vaguely for ten minutes about nothing, then he took me outside and offered me a cigarette.

'I don't smoke, Gerard,' I said.

'Well, that's really positive. I'm glad you quit.'

'I quit years ago—well before I first came to see you for advice about my problem with online Scrabble, Gerard. An addiction, by the way, I am yet to overcome. Of course, now I click on the dicks of a XXX app instead of triple-word scores, but this is beside the point. I just want to know how to live now.'

'I don't fucking know,' said Gerard. 'I'm not over my divorce yet. Nobody is. You never get over it. You've just got to do something different, I suppose. Do something different, and pretend that is *growing*.'

Gerard told me to return home and contact three people to whom I was close for a suggestion on what different thing I should do to help me grow.

I called my mother. She told me to come and live at her place. This was generous, but unfeasible, as my mother and I have not only lived in separate states for more than twenty years, but have had cause to call for intervention during several of those holidays in which we found ourselves reunited. When I reminded her of the Christmas of '04 and her appeal for help to local police, she told me to travel, like that lady from *Eat, Pray, Love*.

'I've seen her on the television,' said my mother. 'I think she mentioned this "growing" you're so keen on.'

I considered travel from the place where things had 'been bad for a while'. I thought about the sexual encounter with the Tuscan youth, the spiritual encounter with the elderly yogi, the consumer encounter with the Laotian tailor who'd knock me out a new closet of clothes for the price of a First-World sandwich.

I considered the possibility that I would return home changed and full of wisdom. I considered the possibility that I would bore the blind shit out of all with stories about my Astounding Personal Growth.

'Everyone is so at peace in India! They have so little but are so wise and happy!'

I looked into this future and saw that I had not 'found' myself but had completely lost my marbles. I had left them at an orientalist bargain sale filled with a people so impoverished

I felt able to buy back my dignity at cost. I had not cured my misery by holidaying in somebody else's. I had just outsourced my hope.

Poor mad, boring Helen, they would say. Travel has not broadened her mind. It has flattened her conversation.

'I learned so much about honouring the human spirit in Uttar Pradesh!' I said, over-enunciating Uttar Pradesh so that every sensible person I knew would make plans to be busy the next time I called.

I couldn't trust my custody of this travel wisdom; I would only come off like a whirring racist who'd taken a theme-park walk in someone else's cut-price shoes. I'd sound as though I believed these divorce-travel nations existed purely to provide *me* with a therapeutic path. I'd sound as though I numbly thought these 'colourful' places were built chiefly for the cure of my grief. My First-World grief cut fresh from sudden separation. Or, rotten from gradual separation as was apparently the case because, you know, 'things had been bad for a while'.

But I did not want to travel and, in fact, could not travel for several reasons. First, I didn't have the money. Second, I couldn't find my passport because this house was a loveless mess. Third, I believed that leaving my home in order to find myself was a deeply flawed idea. I was right *there*, somewhere, and I knew that I needed to look.

Public Service Announcement: When you are lost, you should remain in one place. This is good advice not only for newly dumped persons but for hikers, and for those who have taken hallucinogenic drugs and found them disagreeable.

*

'I am too dead inside to travel,' I told my mother. When someone you have long loved leaves, it does feel a bit like a death. Or, if not death (which, however unpleasant, probably comes, even to the atheist, with a hope for a slide into glory), then it feels *still*. Absolutely still.

It's as though the weather itself has ceased to exist; the force and the context in which you'd lived is gone. There is no longer a sun to lift your mood or a storm that will ruin your plans. There's just no weather. My single, airless ambition was to find the weather again.

Some dumped people are sure they can feel the weather again if only they travel to find it. Perhaps they *can*. Perhaps they *will* find it in the dappled sun of a Tuscan cock-forest. And best of luck to these people. *Buona fortuna*! If I felt for a minute that I could have that shimmering future, I would find the means and will to travel. I would visit Signor Marco and his blazing jizz-torch and warm myself with the young fires, I am told, that still burn for women of my age in southern Europe. But, I knew I couldn't personally expect to find the weather in any climate zone. For me, there just wasn't any more weather.

Instead, I elected to stay in my own nation and find my own storms. I would not travel to Italy. Or India. Or, for the moment, anywhere further than the lavatory.

I wouldn't travel and I wouldn't have my consciousness lit up, either. I just wanted it dimmed, and thoughts of spiritual growth and foreign penises and new dresses were exhausting. 'Be free!' 'Love fully!' 'Dress like a queen at paupers' prices!' These conclusions and the road to their international encounter could all fuck right off.

I would find a new way to feel the old sun and rain on my skin. I really would.

*

I texted Celine:

Helen: My psychologist says I need to ask three people what I should do to 'grow'. Notwithstanding my reasonable fear that you will answer me with something absurd, I am asking you to be one of these persons.

Celine: I am sending you my limited Whore edition of *The Secret*.

Helen: Whore.

Next I called my friend Ameera. She offered to help me to convert to Islam should I care to. This was, in fact, fairly tempting, as (a) I had developed an aversion to alcohol some time back due to life with a hard-drinkin' woman, and (b) this new faith could give real heft to the arguments I was having in the XXX app about US military interventions. But, as I know I'm no great shakes as a joiner, and even less as a scholar of virtue, I declined.

'That's probably good for me, Helen. We Muslims have such a bad reputation already; you'll only make things worse.' She then told me to read Karl Marx, of whom she knew me to be an erratic fan.

Ameera, who had taught Classical Marxism at university, said I should resume my political interest to a point where it became so consuming I overlooked the matter of my private pain entirely in favour of the public sort.

A topic as large as the means of production and a book as big as *Capital* can make a girl shrink down to almost nothing. The ideology. The superstructure. The base. These things can become a humbling Holy Trinity before which we are comfortably nothing. Or, at least, no more than an effect of history.

Revolutionary communism seemed like the most reasonable way to 'grow', until I received a text:

Celine: Look, you KNOW I am just trying to troll you out of suicidal thinking, you dumb whore. And you KNOW I have respect for the counselling process. I've been a fan for years. So, I've been thinking about it and I think you should just 'grow' in the way that I know you want to, which is by getting properly nailed.

Helen: You mean, nailed like the rotten wooden harlot that I am?

Celine: Ya, Schmoopy. Just go on a lot of dates.

I *would* go on a lot of dates—and this is that account. And I am sorry in advance, but I have no better means to describe the interior of a broken heart than this. All I have is a very rough map that shows one dodgy way out of it. Please consult your physician before attempting any part of this dreadful program.

6

Fortyish hours, one bad cinematic metaphor and thirty-seven deleted Facebook posts since she left
Perhaps you have seen the film *The Shawshank Redemption*. If so, one of its best-known scenes will dispose you to an understanding of my attitude on this, the second terrible morning.

If you haven't seen this movie, I apologise for the spoiler. If you have seen it, I apologise for spoiling any good memory of it that you may have. Either way, if you do not wish to associate the vision of a man crawling through a sewage pipe with break-ups, perhaps just skip ahead.

This is what happens in the movie: Tim Robbins, a wrongly accused murderer, surfaces to freedom after years of confinement utterly covered in shit. Well, that's how a dumped and cheated-on person feels. Obviously, we don't crawl through a pipe full of actual poop, but a break-up is a pipe filled with reeking betrayal. Which I imagine is nearly as bad as shit.

It may be clear to cinemagoers that my analogy doesn't last beyond the poop scene. Tim has a shower and adjusts quickly to the freedom he's been planning for years. I, fresh from the foul tunnel and with no plans, could do nothing but cause offence.

Written records of this second morning recall my stink. I did what I earnestly recommend that no one newly released from love does: I hinted at my deep, so terribly deep, pain all over Facebook.

> **Helen Razer:** 6.45 a.m. I am alone.

> **Helen Razer:** 6.45 a.m. There is nothing for me now but death.

> **Helen Razer:** 6.46 a.m. WHY?!

These were among my many sorry status updates, which I had blocked the ex from viewing but kept conspicuously available to everybody else.

> **Public Service Announcement:** If you have been newly dumped, try not to speak much, and write even less. And get the fuck off social media.

I had long despised the tendency in others to VagueBook and rarely was I more tempted to un-friend than when I read something cryptic like 'I forgive you, but I can never trust you again', or 'Please hold our family in your thoughts' with no further explanation.

I had thought of these persons as self-involved time-wasters. *If you have some terrible news to give, give it*, I would say to the screen. Don't leave me to wonder if you're about to kill yourself, perish of cancer or otherwise fall off your perch. I had supposed that if someone was emotionally strong enough to court this kind of public sympathy, then they really didn't require it at all.

Well, the morning after the morning after she left me, I reconsidered. Not all of these people are devious, I thought. While there certainly are those in the habit of soliciting anxiety, there are many more who are just sick of crying alone. Sometimes we need to cry with someone else.

So I posted dozens of bad haikus to sorrow. Even at one point, I believe, a Metallica lyric remembered from my youth. Then I deleted what copyright violation I had posted, leaving those users who had seen an urgent flicker of distress even more muddled than they would have been by a more enduring call for help.

I regret to report that I also uploaded several chiaroscuro self-portraits of my half-naked self on the floor in tears.

Public Service Announcement: Get off Facebook.

These received a creditable volume of 'likes', which I attribute not to pity alone but in part to my instant post-separation weight loss. Which is common, nearly always becoming and, if we don't count full custody of a cat named Eleven, really the only good part of getting dumped.

Posts like mine have now become quite commonplace. Private grief has been largely lost in our era and replaced by conspicuous tantrums. Our best feelings fall into silence and the worst just won't shut up. It's not great that we make such a racket these days, but it can be useful. I crowd-sourced the closest compassion. For me, Facebook became like Uber, but for sympathy.

I wanted to cry in front of someone. Digital innovation brought me a helper named Maddie.

Maddie had seen some of my public rubbish and petitioned me to pick through it by private message. I told her I was 'fucking desperate', which was accurate. She said she'd be right 'round.

I didn't know that much about Maddie at all. I did know she was an occasional writer and awfully keen on feminist statistics.

I had only met Maddie in real life twice. On the first occasion, which was at an art exhibition, she had recited the average depressing ratio of male to female painters hung in the great European galleries. We saw each other again at a meeting for the journalists' union where she recited the average depressing ratio of male to female bylines on the front pages of newspapers. I considered reminding her that no one purchased newspapers anymore, and that art galleries were often places where old ideas went to die, and I couldn't imagine why our gender would want to claim lifeless territory, etc. But she was a sweet girl whose wardrobe of ironic sheath dresses and go-go boots had lifted my spirits, so I said nothing at all.

I am glad that I said nothing. Although frequently preoccupied with depressing statistics, Maddie had been an agreeable presence on Facebook and I often enjoyed her reports. She was agreeable, too, when she arrived at my house quite early that morning. 'You need some biscuits,' she had told me by message and, good to her promise, arrived with a batch of homemade ginger snaps, which were covered with an actual gingham napkin, such as one sees in lifestyle cookbooks but very rarely in the wild.

Although I was not able to eat Maddie's baked goods due to radical sobbing, I was very grateful for the care with which they had been produced. And, I eventually became grateful for the detailed post-dump dating advice Maddie offered.

Maddie was a fixer. Although she had not yet been successful in dismantling the patriarchy and/or equalising the front pages of world press, she was determined to fix my grief.

'What,' she asked as she removed a greaseproof bag to make a place to sit on my sofa, 'would make you feel better right now? Tell me and I'll help you find it.'

I answered, 'Yoga class,' which was bullshit. I dislike yoga and all allied activity undertaken by women who have so much time for leisure they can afford to squander it lying on the floor listening to someone yabber in fake Sanskrit while hardly burning any calories at all. But 'yoga class' was the first thing that came to mind.

When I realised Maddie had plans that required more from me than sobbing 'WHY?' I wanted her to fuck right off to feminist land. I decided that I would pretend to ready myself for yoga class. She would leave and I would learn if Eleven liked ginger snaps. Her good spirits were welcome on the internet but very demanding in real life.

But Maddie was a better student of others than I had supposed. She said, 'Girl, you're so full of shit.' She said she knew that I was the sort about as likely to be calmed by yoga as the women of al-Nusra might have been by enforced participation in the Miss Universe competition, or something else quite funny, and she demanded to know, 'What do you really want?'

'Death,' I said.

'Shut up.'

'To watch *The Shawshank Redemption*.'

'No, you don't,' said Maddie. 'Besides which, it's sexist.' (This may be true. I'm not sure. You'd have to ask another serious feminist.)

'Okay. You know how you're one of those sex-positive feminists?' I said.

'Yes,' she replied.

'Well, I think I want some positive feminist sex.'

'Great!' said Maddie, and offered to introduce me to a friend of a friend called Ines, a pretty pansexual and Head Sleepwear

Designer for a well-known ladies' chain store. Actually, I'd met Ines at a few Gay Baby-naming ceremonies. She had a sexy lisp and dressed for the tastes of a naughty mid-century man.

I did take Ines's number, but not because I thought she would have sex with me, or even that I wanted to have sex with her. I took it because I was in urgent need of a new sleeping garment.

'Actually, I think I want positive feminist sex with a man.'

Maddie was a heterosexual feminist, but a feminist nonetheless. And so, the displeasure on her face was plain as soon as I uttered this urge. She was disappointed I had abandoned woman-only activity.

'Hm,' she said.

I felt obliged to reassure this feminist that I had not shunned the embrace of my sisters forever. And this moment of civility, my first in days, forced me to think about men, and why I wanted sex with one of them.

I have never endured a preference for the company of just one sex. But now, a man was what I craved, and I really couldn't explain this to myself, much less Maddie, who seemed so disappointed she needed an explanation. So I was forced to think.

Perhaps, given that a woman had just dumped me, I had a need for distance from the feminine physique? That explanation was plausible, but I couldn't offer it to a feminist, as it sounded sexist to ascribe the qualities of one woman to all. But, still, vagina. Ugh.

Perhaps we could say that sex with men was easier than sex with women? I decided to elaborate on this idea of men as simpler partners.

'Sex with men is over in more of a hurry,' I said. 'Sex with women tends to go on forever, especially on first dates.'

This is actually true. Sapphic sex can often be a case of 'Your turn, my turn' and recalls an all-night game of basketball, only with orgasms instead of points. Half-time entertainment does not involve dancing, either, but listening to the story of someone's childhood trauma. Or eating a wheat-free tortilla with pH-neutral beans. In short, first-date lesbianism is a young and fit woman's game. Neither my ageing jaw nor my patience were up to it.

'So, you are saying that sex with men is quicker, less meaningful, and therefore more transactional?' she said, hopefully. Maddie was nearly as disappointed by my refusal to be A Lesbian as the men on the XXX app, although for different reasons.

'Yes! I don't want involvement, Maddie. I want to make an exchange. I want efficient sex that ends when someone comes. Because, frankly, I'm both horny and exhausted.'

Although pacified by my account of men as single-use vaginal wipes, Maddie still wasn't *entirely* pleased. She admired women-only enterprise, even if this enterprise was pleasure and even if it did mean a little extra work. Maddie herself was a tireless worker for the cause of female emancipation, showing active dedication to raising funds for women-only spaces and the like. I am pretty sure she thought the least a non-activist like me could do was eat a little muff.

But the matter of desire, unlike women's housing, is not political. Sex can never be governed by good intentions, as my newly waxed ex-girlfriend would probably concede.

I said, 'I do imagine I'll see women again,' to reassure her. Then I said, 'Sexuality is a spectrum, you know,' which is something I'd heard other young feminists say. I knew that 'fluidity' was a popular theme with serious feminists, so I took it up.

'I think I need to be more fluid,' I said.

Maddie said, 'Right,' and opened her MacBook, bringing almost the same resolve to the provision of penis as she did to the maintenance of women's safe houses.

'Let's find you some cock, then.'

'Do you think I could get someone to fuck me? I mean, I haven't seen Eleni the beauty therapist in months and I suspect I look a fright.'

'Don't worry,' Maddie said. 'You are effortlessly stunning.'

You should know that I am not 'effortlessly stunning'. Give me forty-five minutes in a bathroom and I'll produce 'moderately presentable', but nothing more. 'Effortlessly stunning' does not legitimately describe the appearance of most humans, much less one who has been dumped in the middle of summer. I have selfies from the period and 'week-old offal in a nightgown' comes much closer to capturing the vision.

In the effort not to look like budget meats, I called Eleni and made the appointment for the afternoon. It was not yet lunchtime and Maddie had decided that the day had sufficient stuff left in it to unite me with one and possibly two persons in possession of a functional penis. Clearly, a dolphin was required.

'We're going to write you a good, traditional dating profile,' she said. 'Like on the old-timey internet. Not one of those young people's location-based sex apps.'

She explained that I was vulnerable. Too vulnerable for Tinder or for the hard stink of the filthy XXX application I had previously tried. 'Get off those things. Stop looking for the penis icon in your postcode. Proximity can't be your only criterion,' she said.

'We'll do it this way, and if you have to travel a bit to meet your penis, at least it will be attached to someone who probably shares your taste in film.'

I may have been too *vulnerable*, but probably, to be honest, also a little too *old* for the instant fix of the mobile-only application. She wanted me to *slow down* and think for a minute and jolly well act my age.

'You can still access this one on your phone,' she said. 'It's an app, but less impulse-friendly than Tinder. No "dick near me" coordinates.'

Maddie was right. I had looked at Tinder. It seemed very much like Uber, but for sexually transmitted infections.

Slow down. Take a minute.

She asked me to think, slowly and specifically, about what we'd write in the yet-to-be-published dating profile she guaranteed would have me meeting one or two more-or-less suitable persons with penis inside a day. I explained to her that there were hundreds of men on the XXX app who didn't really care to read a profile or discuss cinema at all. Surely this was a waste of time and I should simply dress as a sheep.

'You are not,' she said, 'twenty-five anymore. You are in your forties. And a bit of a grump.' Her point being that I was, both generationally and genetically, disinclined to be tolerant when meeting new people.

Besides which, she said, 'You are a known snob who would have a fit if you met some bloke whose favourite band was Coldplay.'

I couldn't argue with her logic. I *was* a terrible snob, and so was my vagina.

'Come on, Sugar Tits,' she said. 'You're the copywriter. Advertise yourself.'

There are those who manage this sort of self-promotion with ease. But I approached it as I approach most activity: with crippling reflection. In any case, I had never been particularly good at advertising. I would never be an in-demand copywriter because my work, as some important tool at an important agency assessed during interview, was 'Edgy, but *bad* edgy.' He said that my bad attitude would prevent me from ever writing, or enacting, a slogan half as good as 'Just Do It'.

I know there are vigorous persons who live their lives to the motivation of 'Just Do It', and they even sometimes win. I am simply not one of them. I tend to think at length before committing to an intimate or professional action. This does not mean that I act wisely, or even that I act at all. It does mean, however, I am painfully conscious that the 'Just Do It' advertising slogan was inspired by the final words of a convicted murderer, Gary Gilmore, as he faced the firing squad in the United States.

When I mentioned this to Maddie she told me to shut up, cease all thoughts of homicide—reminding me that women are more likely to be brutally killed by their husbands than by internet suitors, which was an oddly uplifting application of a depressing feminist statistic—and to have a think about what I might like to say about myself.

'I am a 43-year-old newly divorced chicken carcass,' I suggested.

Maddie was having none of it.

'What shall we say you do for a living? Writer?'

'I reproduce history's hopeless cycle of material desperation.'

'No.'

'I exchange my labour for money.'

Maddie, who was in the journalists' union, said that this one was not great, but okay, she'd let it through.

Due, perhaps, to her many years of volunteer counselling for frontline women's services, Maddie had developed a knack for psychological massage. At first it seemed she was just being annoyingly perky in demanding that I describe myself well to an audience. Very Optimitorium. Then it struck me, after I had written 'Sexually ambivalent middle-aged crank' and 'Infrequent showerer' and other palaver she rejected, that she was applying a form of therapy.

The composition of a dating profile is not just a lark. It can be a *treatment.*

I remembered that some years before, back when I was working on some commercial copy for a seniors' dating start-up venture, I spoke with a lady who had completed a postdoctoral thesis on internet dating. An interesting subject to encounter in this dull line of commercial work, she had focused particularly on the over-55s.

'They learn to write the self,' she had said as I transcribed it. 'They write themselves into the kind of partner that they would like to be.'

'At first, they dislike writing about themselves,' she went on. 'They tell bad jokes and use poor grammar and they do everything they can to avoid a reliable and clear self-description. Then, after a while, they begin to enjoy it. They know it's good for them. Writing a profile is good, therapeutic work.'

She had read me some of her favourite senior profiles and these struck me as really warm or funny, or both. I looked for these fragments on my laptop and read them to Maddie:

I have always enjoyed reading a good Whodunnit, and I have collected these until there's no space left. But I'd clear them out in a second if it meant I could solve the mystery of love. I'm 72 years bold, a widower and in pretty decent nick, thanks to three of the world's fastest grandchildren. I am a Lions Club Member, an avid gardener and a swimmer. My life is as crammed as my bookshelf, but there's always space for a happy conclusion. Ladies 65 and over, message me and we'll see if we can't come to the end together.

Yes, I'm a cranky man with an aversion to loud chewing noises and the thought of children on my lawn. No, I will never leave your side.

I'm a loud septuagenarian minx who drinks Chablis by the drum. I have been known to wheel my Yorkie in a stroller. But if you look past the dog lady and ignore the white wine pong, you'll see that my jugs still stand up on their own and that us two old fools belong in the sack. (That's you and me, baby. Not my two jugs, AKA Cagney and Lacey. No separating those girls.)

Maddie was moved, and as she began to cry I found that I could finally stop. As I had outsourced my tears, I began to wonder a little more rationally if I could do what these seniors had in their profiles. It couldn't be *that* different for me, I thought. Perhaps my elders were prone to describe their physical selves in profile less often as 'hot', as Maddie had generously advised I do, and more as 'not yet insulin resistant'. Otherwise, Dr Over-55's advice, which came back to me that morning, held: Write the self. Write the self that you want to be with others.

I stared at the field: describe yourself. Others on the site Maddie had showed me wrote, 'Into sports' or 'Likes a laugh' or 'Compassionate towards my fellow humans'. I couldn't think of anything save for 'Ageing poseur with possible interest in spanking.' I remembered that my academic lady had said that shitty jokes were initially quite common.

You start out laughing. You end up thinking about the self you want to be with others. That's what she advised. And then you can laugh again with others.

'You have to write and rewrite in life,' she had said. 'This is how I finished my thesis and this is how I, also an over-55 dater, got myself not only laid but sane.'

The part of the dating process her survey respondents often found the most personally profitable was not actually going out and finding senior sex by internet, but the act itself of writing a profile. 'Writing can give you time to think,' she said. 'It gives you time to think about how best to be with others.'

(This is absolutely not true for the kind of writing demanded by discount advertising.)

Some of the interviewees reported that the act of creating themselves in text helped them connect better back in the physical world. One lady had said that even though she ended up finding dates the old-school way, through friends and family and the like, the practice of editing a profile had really helped her confidence. She knew a little more of who she was, and who she wanted to be, after writing it down twenty times.

None of these findings were useful for the shit portfolio copy I was commissioned to write, but they were very useful to recall that morning with Maddie, who, as a very upbeat person even when crying, was interested to hear me read all this Oprah-style self-actualisation aloud.

'The internet asks us questions like, "How would you describe yourself?" and "What are you looking for?" and when we answer them, we do so not only to find someone, but to find ourselves,' said Dr Over-55.

I recited this from my laptop to Maddie, who said, 'You should answer these questions. And, perhaps for the first time, Sugar Tits, you should give honest answers.'

It was daytime TV in here. I shouldn't have been surprised if someone had said, 'EVERYBODY GETS A CAR!' when we'd finished weeping. Maddie would have driven home in a new Ford with a Deepak Chopra decal.

Maddie showed me some other good, readable profiles, including that charming one she had written herself years before. It was sweet and as honest as an act of online-reputation management could be. 'I want to learn you really well,' it said. 'I want to learn you better than I ever learned anything.'

This writing had provided her with a good feminist husband. And, she said, the act of writing had helped her ready herself not only for this fulfilling marriage but for the several liaisons that preceded it and the happiness that continued to flow.

'I know you're not looking for love, like I was,' said Maddie. 'But the same rules apply. Be honest in your approach so that others can approach you honestly.'

Maddie had been fluent, but I was creatively constipated. I was suffering a very bad case of mocking detachment. I wrote like I was only half present and, even then, there entirely on a whim. I had acquired the internet's pervasive voice of indifference. I was snarky or I was smarmy, and when I used a superlative like 'brilliant' or 'great', no one could know what I meant.

The voice of the internet is so non-stop it can no longer be certain of its mood or its meaning. It is never reflective. Things become one thing or the other thing at such speed they then become nothing at all. On the internet, we are always outraged or enthusiastic; we are dangerously happy or bereaved.

> **Public Service Announcement:** Slow down when you are looking for sex on the internet. Slow down to the point you might actually connect with a meaningful penis.

Tell us what you are looking for. Others wrote, 'Nothing serious' or 'Not one-degree south of absolute passion' or 'Polyamorous Kink companion'. I wrote, 'Recently bathed human', 'Partner in complex hate-fucking', and 'Distraction from suicidal ideation'. All of which are things I meant and didn't mean at all. They were self-distancing non-thoughts: the sort produced by the internet.

I was edgy, but *bad* edgy. The words and the message, which was, in this case, myself, just didn't coincide.

Maddie, who had socially useful places to be, finally allowed me to publish 'Baffling old woman with reasonable cans seeks more-or-less sober life-form who genuinely dislikes Coldplay.' Which was as daytime TV as I was ever going to get. She also let me keep the stupid screen name of MidLifeISIS, which I found hilarious.

She wiped my face of sick and replaced this with a little powder. She took a few snaps, filtered and uploaded them and cheered as I hit 'publish'. She said that she was off to the, I don't know, Women in Exceptionally Bad Circumstances steering committee, but that she'd call to check on me in a few hours, when I would be preparing for the assignations she felt confident I could make in that time.

'You'll be stuffed with penis,' she said as she sped off in her Honda Civic to sort out gender inequality.

That day, baffling old woman with reasonable cans sought a more-or-less sober life-form who genuinely dislikes Coldplay.

7

Forty-five hours and one dating profile since she left
'Fuck u, Coldplay is awesome.'

Things really hadn't started out well.

As it turns out, a declared contempt for Coldplay can be cause for a great deal of rage. 'Fuck u, Coldplay is awesome' was typical of the rejoinders to my profile. I knew that the supermarkets had done their work.

If you have not noticed before, you certainly will now: the contemporary mid-range supermarket plays the music of Coldplay, or music much like Coldplay's, almost constantly. At well-known, middle-market supermarkets, we can hear moderately sad songs of the type at all hours. Discount supermarkets play energetic pop. High-end gourmet supermarkets play jazz or children's choirs murdering age-inappropriate popular songs at dawdling tempo and terrifying pitch. But the big brand stores elect to play music in this Coldplay key of tolerable desperation. They really do. *Listen.*

I know from my horrid work that it is consumer research that leads Western retailers to broadcast this refined white misery. Somewhere, a focus group has answered the question 'What music makes you feel sad enough to want a chocolate but not to actually kill yourself?' with 'Coldplay'. Marketing experts have learned that bands like Coldplay, REM and U2 make many of us crave a cure to an undefined pain. We become certain of the remedy but forget the nature of the ill. (Bono is a dick.)

When we hear this stuff in a supermarket, we are inclined to believe that the thing that it makes us crave is available on the shelves. I know that I have purchased napkin rings as the direct result of hearing U2's 'With or Without You'. Bono is a dick.

This is a very particular kind of music. It's a slow, emotional drone that evokes a hint of our everyday pain. But it also fails to describe this pain so adequately that we might actually pause to investigate its source. Coldplay makes pain seem beautiful and manageable. Coldplay means we never stare pain in the face. We experience it briefly, then we are wont to shop our way out of it.

Pain-relief shopping is not always a terrible idea, by the by. If I'd had a little extra money during my break-up, I would have done well to throw it at my pain. I do not consider 'retail therapy' a particularly immoral pursuit in a world so impossibly predicated on shite, and, certainly, it can be a remedy for distress, even if it is also the poison. Buy some stuff. It's no big deal. Sometimes when I am anxious, I stare at online kitchenware stores for hours and bring myself to happiness with napkin rings.

But I was broke, Brynlee-free and temporarily unable to write any profitable sentence. I did not have the means to afford any mollifying tableware, so I wrote copy on the internet for no wages about how much I loathed Coldplay. Coldplay and the devious marketing strategies upon which their treacly whine was slathered.

I thought I was being rather funny. I kept adding to my profile on the theme of Coldplay-hate, and, after a few edits, I had ruined all of Maddie's good supervision. In the section that asked, 'What do you dream of?', I said, 'Coldplay dying in a freak aromatherapy spa accident.' This made me laugh, but apparently failed to tickle a man in the 39–45 age range who asked, 'Whats ur problem with coldplay ugly Dyke??'

(Again, with the forcefully redundant capitalisation.)

I tried to parse this difficult sentence. The proximity of Coldplay to a slur that was both sexist *and* homophobic *and* made by a straight man who liked Coldplay suggested either (a) that it was unfeminine not to enjoy this music, or (b) that the band was somehow very butch. Which is clearly untrue. Coldplay is as convincingly masculine as I was effortlessly stunning.

This message was one of many pro-Coldplay assaults whose basis I found difficult to identify and, therefore, fairly fascinating. The passionate love for Coldplay was both unfathomable and unexpected. In an effort to understand it, I kept adding to my profile vignettes about the grisly, alternative therapy-related murders of the band. I left the drummer for dead in a float tank and the bass player brutally finished off in a bee-sting therapy session gone awry. I did it because, of course, I hate Coldplay. Even more than I hate U2, who are so obviously naïve it's almost endearing—but, shit, Bono is a dick.

In any case, it wasn't just because I hate Coldplay. I also wanted to see how much one's taste could affect one's emotional future.

People, including myself, can be very touchy when it comes to their favourite things. Taste, as Maddie had counselled, is really quite important. The preferences and aversions detailed on these dating profiles meant much more to me, even a person quite aware that taste functioned to reveal nothing nobler about its bearer than social class, than they should.

For example, in performing a 'female seeking female' search, I saw a cruelly beautiful brunette of my approximate age. Goodness, she was gorgeous—she looked quite a bit like Ines, the saucy sleepwear designer. Her mildly censored naked profile picture showed the sort of unfeasible infinity figure otherwise seen only in the notebooks of masturbating sci-fi teen cartoonists, very rarely here on earth in three dimensions.

Hers was the kind of geometry that could start Lord Byron on a curvilinear tear. *Poetry*. It was a public service to show it. It should be a summary offence to conceal it. I reconsidered this whole yawning need for cock thing and prepared to message the author of the undulating vision.

A picture may be worth a thousand words, but only if none of those words gather to form such sentences as: 'I hate talking about issues, zzz, YOLO!' Or, 'Nicolas Cage 4 LYF.' I like issues and I dislike being forced to think about Nicolas Cage—or, for that matter, the meaning of internet acronyms. Taste would not permit me to message the woman with the infinity figure and the careless abbreviations. Taste was some important bullshit.

Several people had messaged me on the matter of taste, though. Chiefly to tell me 'You blow'. I was so captivated by how a mildly comic reference to a mediocre band could provoke so much real ire from so many middle-aged people. I mean, honestly, you *pussies*.

Eventually, I was no longer amused by this Coldplay-related butt-hurt. The joke had become unfunny, even to MidLifeISIS.

Two hours in and I had no prospects. This, as I had been led to suppose, was a long interval for a female internet dater to endure alone. And yes, I *know* that it was all my fault.

I resolved once more to follow the pointers from Dr Over-55's study and Maddie's frank counsel. I would erase my nastiness. I would write measured sentences about myself and my hopes. I would be considerate but frank, needful but self-assured. I would earn this date, and I would appreciate it, based on a plain advertisement of the self.

I revised the stories about Coldplay and their deaths by acupressure massage. I began to replace them with candid and simple accounts of my state and my need for company. I felt sorry that my mean and derisive mood, which had been brewing for two days, or ten years, was now giving others cause for pain. Even if it was dumb pain acquired at supermarkets. Who was I to judge others for their ignorance? I had recently managed to overlook months of my faithless spouse's hand-jobs in the shed. Talk about ignorance.

I began to type into the profile field:

It has been ~~almost forty-eight hours three months~~ four weeks since my partner left me with the words 'I need to grow' and since then I have had little to do but ~~masturbate weep into matte-finish floorboards~~ think.

And I think that what I want is to move from ~~the floor~~ solitude to genuine and accommodating interest in my fellows.

~~Also, I would really like to get banged.~~

To this end, I have decided to date, and to do this with an attitude of minimum expectation and of maximum respect.

~~Please bang me.~~

If you are neither biologically old enough to be my parent nor young enough to be my issue, I cordially invite all comers to ~~my muff~~ a casual assignation.

I am ready to embrace all sorts of people. However. I should say that I have, ahem, an 'issue' with addiction. Particularly alcoholism. I can't be around it. And I've an issue with those to whom it has not yet occurred that the material conditions of existence determine, in large part, the shape of any person's life.

Yes, I know. I am looking for a moderate drinker from the material left.

Good luck with that unicorn, MidLifeISIS.

Anyhow. If you are a racist, an essentialist, or have ever uttered the sentence, 'You know, that David Icke really makes a lot of sense', please do not respond.

And, please do not respond if you are looking for a wife. I do not believe I can cohabit again. ~~I do not think I could live with the fear that someone so close to me could hate me so much~~. Also, I don't want to reproduce; and I'm ~~43~~ 41 so my eggs are probably powdered, anyhow.

I don't want to consume you whole. But I would like to ~~to get banged you to buy me a decent dinner as I am fucking broke having recently quit my job~~ see where things lead.

Of course, you should know before accepting my invitation that I am really—despite a genuine desire to be better—quite a tit. And I'm not just saying that as a sort of coy double-bluff that will have you refusing with a 'No, no! You are clearly lovely.' I'm not. I'm awful. And if we are to have any hope of a second date, it's probably pretty important that you are a bit awful, too.

This is who I am. I am a sometimes needy, often overweening, wildly affectionate harridan. I can't hold my tongue, but I will keep your confidence. I can't suspend judgement, but I can excuse your sin. I often think that I am right, but I will be thrilled when you can prove me wrong. I am full of love. I am full of revulsion. I am leaking with compassion. I am the world's worst snob.

Oh, and I can't eat barbecue chicken in company.

Anyhow. If you're up for a meeting in flattering light, as I am ~~43~~ ~~42~~ 41, then do be in touch.

Before I had published these changes, I noticed a few more message alerts. The subjects indicated more of the 'Fuck u Coldplay' type. But then I saw one titled 'Workers to Power! Death to Coldplay' and this amused and buoyed me greatly.

Without pausing to publish the extended mix of my *cri de cœur*, I clicked on to the note. It was from Anticathexis, a 41-year-old man of athletic build seeking women less than ten kilometres from MidLifeISIS, a woman of indeterminate age looking for cock and in possession of a newly slender silhouette.

Anticathexis: Hello, MidLifeISIS. While it is normally true that I find that the declaration of cultural likes and dislikes has no work other than to filter social class, I also hate Coldplay. I hate Coldplay so much that I am powerless not to admire your revulsion. I am also powerless not to admire your photograph which, to be very clear, I do not hate but rather fancy. Who, after all, can say they do not appreciate the thought of a cantankerous blonde preaching reasonable hate from her threadbare—was it blue?—sleep attire? Perhaps if you are not moved to Coldplay-level disgust by my own series of bashfully artistic photographs, we can meet and plot to assassinate Chris Martin? I suggest that we poison his urine health tonic and/or feed him some lunch rich in gluten. In solidarity, Anticathexis, more plainly known as John. I would include a smiling emoticon but suspect you'd disapprove.

I read this glory seven times just to be certain it was real and not the product of secret collaboration between my ego and my id.

8

Forty-six hours and one single moment of hope since she left

The novice online dater is likely to face many obstacles in her attempts to secure an actual offline date. It may be that chief among these is the impediment of herself.

As soon as the conversation with Anticathexis had started, I did all that I could to forestall its end. I just wanted to write to him forever. Such a blithe, left-wing and mutually congratulatory exchange as I anticipated we'd have, could never be bettered, I felt, by any physical meeting. All I wanted was the pleasure of this preamble and none of the pain of interrupting it with an actual date.

MidLifeISIS: Good afternoon, John, and warm thanks for the invitation to view your gallery of moody self-portraits.

These, despite their debt to the miserablist work of Dorothea Lange, seem to reveal a fanciable man. That this miserable but fanciable man has selected a Freudian term as his screen name (I promise, I didn't need to Google it! Okay, I did, but not much) and answered the profile question of 'What are you usually doing on a Friday night?' with 'Hating self', 'Attending a live reading of *Ulysses*' or 'Huffing paint down the car park with me bruvs' only amplifies my interest. I am currently a great fan of bathos and I have long been very interested in good-looking men who despise themselves a bit. It always saves me the trouble. My thanks again for your note. Helen. Semi-colon with parenthesis used to suggest the wink of future familiarity.

I waited somewhere between an hour and seventeen years for a response.

Anticathexis: Helen. I also send gratitude that is as warm as this very warm day. A day so warm, I am currently driving to the beach to escape it. J. Slightly crazy emoticon represented by a colon followed by a lower-case 'p'.

After such a reasonable rush of words and our shared declaration of probable desire, this last short and busy and late message was one I found difficult to take. Then again, I found food, the need to urinate and breathing hard to take, so my sensitivity threshold *may* have been a little lower than usual.

I am driving to the beach. Well, la-di-da, 'John'. Did he mean that I should not contact him again soon? Was the advice of his excursion meant to convey unconcern and/or a full schedule, and outdoorsy ways? And how in blazes could he choose an afternoon of sun over online badinage with me? I am very fucking special.

I drafted some replies about my revulsion for the beach and for the men who preferred an entire ocean to feminine harbour, but they all reeked of self-importance and hurt. As I knew that I had effectively managed to reek of nothing but self-importance and hurt for about fifty hours (probably for many thousands of hours before these), I deleted my draft responses. After ten minutes or so, I sent:

> Enjoy all of nature's remaining charm and the best of our city's hypodermic needles.

Five minutes. He did not reply. Fifteen minutes. His presence was registered as 'online', but he did not reply.

I pictured this stranger, whom I had so quickly come to worship and resent, at the beach. This was fairly trying, as all I really had to work with was a few low-resolution photographs, and the knowledge that he was qualified to the postgraduate level and physically 'athletic'.

Public Service Announcement: 'Athletic', I have found, is an online-dating category applied to the bodies of men that can mean anything. From critically manorexic to quite chubby, 'athletic' may represent any type of adult male body, so long as it once performed or still performs or, perhaps, sometimes just views some kind of sport. Possibly including darts.

Look. I know the guy was probably driving and unable to pick up his phone. I also know that there are people who genuinely love the beach and, somehow, find it useful on hot days. Still. Fuck him. Fuck him in his holes. How could he do this to me, who is special? And I became, again, quite potty.

I pottily imagined John's eyes falling upon other women at the beach, possibly from the top of a Freud Penguin Classic. What a wanker. He was reading *Civilisation and Its Discontents*. His superego was drawn to the long, olive limbs of Arty Sandra, which were set against the soft blue Tasman Sea. Therein, Stellan and Junyper were cavorting like immune-compromised flathead and, between their fits of salt allergy, she was tending to their skin with all-natural, all-useless sunscreen.

Such a man, one who photographs himself in dramatic, depression-era light that reveals so little about his actual appearance and everything about his need to be Taken Seriously, is just the sort who would love an artsy mother. Fuck this brief messenger. Fuck you, John. I hope this mild afternoon of genital misconduct with Arty Sandra brings you an embarrassing virus. I hope that you will never know the feel of a vagina like mine, unravished by reusable moon cups and two home births in a spa bath, John.

I know, John, that when you give Sandra her next and most geriatric pregnancy, you will confront immediate regret and fall despondently in love with her midwife. You will move from one woman to another, as you always do. You change the scenery, John. But you never change the script.

Your life will now be lived in a nightmare of complementary medicine and every breath you take will be contorted by rose geranium oil and your complicity with ignorance. Life with Sandra was fetid enough, but now you know, John, just how bad it can really smell. Arachnia uses no deodorant. This doula shuns soap as the evil work of Big Pharma. She tells you each day that there are things They Don't Want You To Know.

Your anti-civilisation life has become a daguerreotype nightmare of conspiracy theory and Paleo eating, John! She doesn't swallow because she says she's semen intolerant. I swallow, John. Well, I have not been previously tested on the matter, but I imagine that I might. Nonetheless, Arachnia has never swallowed nor shaved her legs and, for all your declared feminist principles, you *know* you want a woman who bothers to observe such conventions. A woman, like me, who swallows. Probably. A woman who removes the hair from her legs. Even if only to show that she cares to receive you. As I did once. But do no longer, John. John, I fucking hate you.

Obviously, this fantasy was baneful and unsound, but it did achieve two things. First, I was so disgusted by myself I had a long shower. Next, I made a date for that evening with the only other user who had not yet urged me to die in a fire.

*

RedHot, so called for his birth in the former Soviet Union, was nice looking and functionally literate. He was also, as his profile had it, 'completely down to fuck'. He told me I was pretty and promised me a 'ride' on his 'Big Slavic Cock'.

These were not complicated or long exchanges. The ecstasy of communication was not provided here. But perhaps it was better not to be drawn into such tosh. One falls in love with writing itself and, as seen in the Sandra correspondence, or in the data centres of Google, we all tend to leave an embarrassing document behind if we are not especially careful.

John was the kind of person that could only entice a literature of humiliation from me. I would spend time writing to him and find myself quickly transformed into an unpublished E.L. James.

No one should write when they are horny. There ought to be a law.

I would fix my unhealthy relationship with words and go to meet a man who didn't care for words very much at all. We would leave no written record. We were completely down to fuck.

'Words must serve me,' I wrote on an open document. 'Not I, them'. This happened to be written, I noticed, beneath words that I had served up two nights before:

> When the dazzling smile of youth goes dark, it's time to turn to the high-wattage magic of an adult tooth fairy. Say Bibbidi-Bobbidi BOO to unmagical teeth as the Whitening Wand restores the light for only $39.95 for your first session!

This shit that had met the bills should have been so easy to write. But this discount copy had come to slash my happiness by half. That's 50 per cent off the everyday price. A person less afflicted by the worship of words would just have damn well written words and not sustained so many workplace injuries from them. But I had, in fact, been fairly wounded by words. Words had abused me, I thought. Which was not something I could report to my union.

I knew that I liked to use words for their own sake and had been told often that I *loved* the sound of my own voice. Which is true; my religious ecstasy is communication. It was not true that this allowed a practical approach to online dating. Or to anything much, really.

So I tried to forget John's ephemera and anticipate the real Big Slavic Cock instead. A Big Slavic Cock that would not make me write things. One that would permit undocumented pleasure.

Sex, and not words, in black and white. No shades.

I would meet RedHot that evening. Wordless and waxed. The appointment with Eleni was made.

9

Forty-seven hours and two privacy violations since she left

It is still the case that on bad days I blame John for problems he did not actually cause. Which is not to say that he would not cause me some actual problems. He would. (Did you really think I'd *not* pursue with the stubborn force of US foreign policy someone who sent me a sex terrorism message like his? Sometimes I don't think you 'get' me at all!) But the problem for which I would briefly blame him that day really wasn't his fault.

It is possibly true that if John had answered my messages within a reasonable period instead of making me wait an *actual hour* while he selfishly enjoyed the beach I would not have gone out to the shed again and checked the ex's Facebook account more thoroughly. But it is certainly true that I would have found out about C'arter at some point if it hadn't been that afternoon.

Now, I can't say why the ex hadn't changed her password and, again, I want to remind you that I once sent money to Edward Snowden, or some other noble person exiled for their commitment to internet privacy. But *you* try discovering that someone with a name like C'arter is associated with your just-departed ex and see if you can't help looking.

I was charmed to learn, thanks to the unforgetful internet, that C'arter was very recently known as Carter, and so she had not been catastrophised by her parents but had embarrassed herself.

Naturally, I was delighted by this artless apostrophe. But I was somewhat less delighted to learn that the fortnight C'arter had spent speaking with my ex was sufficient to inspire a declaration of love, gifts from Amazon and a minute-by-minute account of all my elasticised farts.

Everything. Everything I did that could be observed had been reported by my ex in real time to this pretentiously punctuated stranger. There were thousands of words, many of them even more passionate than those exchanged with Arty Sandra. Those that did not optimistically describe the pair's glorious imagined future described my real and miserable recent past. And they did so rather impatiently, sometimes cruelly, and almost always as-it-happened.

My life had become the material for an awful live and private blog. I saw that the ex had paused at the traffic lights on the drive to her uncle's Christmas dinner to write C'arter a message while I was sitting beside her.

'I have the Butthole Surfers turned up max so I can't hear Helen droning on again about federal politics,' she wrote, as *Locust Abortion Technician* sounded even louder than my complaints about tax concessions to the rich.

'I guess I should be nicer to her,' she wrote. 'Because when I leave her for you, she'll never see this family again.'

'Helen is in her blue flannel nightdress *again*.'

'Helen doesn't want to go out to the pub *again*.'

'Helen is asking me to turn down the Goa trance so she can do her dumb work *again*.'

'I swear, she enjoys being a martyr.'

(For those up the back: this last statement was not made entirely without recourse to reality.)

It is unpleasant enough to snoop. It becomes intolerable when the snooping reveals that you have yourself been snooped on. She'd had me under steady surveillance and kept a sedulous record of my faults.

There was some general moaning to C'arter about the tiresome quality of my kisses and my cooking. She found my gardening too methodical and my attachment to disposable disinfectant wipes extreme. Between these tedious facts lay a few fancies. Many of these fibs concerned finance, specifically that I lay about most of the day while she worked much harder for the money, etc.

In her fictional reading of things, I was terrible at sex and at yard work, and this was possibly true. And that I was a terrible provider, which was absolutely not. It's perhaps the only thing I've ever been much chop at. I have never made my lady rich, but I always kept her in tolerable ease.

It was awful to be called a bad wife *and* a bad husband, but the thing that troubled me more than anything was the assault on my blue flannel nightdress.

I really loved that blue nightdress. I'd even named it—Elsa, after a domesticated lioness that is not keen on leaving her cage for the wilderness at the end of an old film about gamekeepers. I'd had Elsa for several seasons and she'd just hit the perfect soft spot between baby harp seal and total collapse so that I couldn't bear the thought of replacing her with something more appropriate to summer. But as I was wearing Elsa now, I found that she no longer provided great comfort. Along with all my most intimate secrets, Elsa had been shredded with C'arter.

Our life together had been diminished and edited and upcycled for this ardent thread.

I wanted to log off. Until the unlikely appearance in this long conversation of a particular word modified in my guts to the texture of ash and I kept reading.

It's a silly word. I feel silly telling you about it. But it's possible you might find some personal use in being told about this silly thing.

The ex and I had, as couples do over time, developed a range of ridiculous names to address each other when no one else was listening. Those things that intimates call each other, like 'Sugar Bear' or 'Fluffetina' or, I don't know, 'Beyoncé my Fiancée'. I saw that the most private one of ours had been disclosed.

The ex had come to call me 'Bunnum', a portmanteau, I guess, of 'bunny' and 'possum', and look, *there she was* using it to address C'arter, a young American woman who she had not yet met beyond electronic networks. 'I think I love you, Bunnum,' she wrote.

Even as the hand-me-down donation of this name conferred a kind of vindication—I was, as far as I knew, its original bearer—it was also, in my view, the most fatal violation. We were over. Over. Didn't matter how.

Well. I say that we were over and I imply that I had arrived at a wise conclusion. And perhaps some portion of me had become terribly wise and resigned. But this portion was deep beneath layers of me, who is, as we now know, nothing if not a dick. So I stayed for a few more rounds of 'truth' on the internet.

There I learned that C'arter was twenty-five, had 'skin like a teen angel' and shared a keen interest with my ex, recently turned forty, in the Myer–Briggs Type Indicator—a form of widely discredited personality testing that makes the work of L. Ron Hubbard seem almost scholarly by contrast. They were both 'INTJ', or something, and therefore among the rarest and most special test-takers on the planet. They had met on an 'INTJ' page, which was full of people congratulating each other identically for their uniqueness.

I had heard about this 'INTJ' malarkey once before when writing copy for a recruitment company's website. I was speaking to one of the company's grumpy MBAs who happened to be particularly cheesed that day by job-selection committees. 'Why do they rely so often on unproven behavioural tests, like that stupid Myer–Briggs?' he asked, as though some shit writer like me would have any satisfying answer. He hated Myer–Briggs. He had told me its popularity in the recruitment sector was due to something psychologists called the 'Barnum Effect'.

The Barnum Effect. Which I will always now misread as the Bunnum Effect.

The promoter PT Barnum famously promised that his shows had 'something for everyone'. So tests like these, which offer all the one-size-fits-most flattering complexity of horoscopes, do the same kind of thing. One broad and becoming description—either of a personality type or a star sign—worked to validate large numbers of naïve people eager to be entertained. In this case, not by Barnum's circus but by stories about themselves. So, large numbers of people, including human resources managers who probably should know better, continued to believe in this unscientific crap, the MBA told me. 'It's just vanity.'

I looked at the page where they had met. Apparently, the 'INTJ' was the very rarest personality type distinguished by 'complexity of character' and the 'unusual range and depth of our talents'. Which is, of course, exactly how most modern people, including me, like to think of ourselves.

C'arter and the ex had great faith in the personality type a few minutes of internet testing had awarded them. Together, they were forging complexity and depth of a type that couldn't even be imagined by a common personality like mine. Which, they had agreed, was probably 'ESFJ'.

I didn't even bother looking that up as I have always had little patience for psychometric bullshit, and in that moment even less for my own pettiness. That was enough snooping.

I finally didn't care to know more or be further tempted to compare my virtues against those of a Bunnum replacement so dubious even Arty Sandra was now looking both tolerable and sane.

I did think about finding C'arter's phone number and telling her she was a slut, and a slut who was not rare but quite undistinguished by talent or complexity of character. I did think about facilitating conversation between her and Arty Sandra, whose intimacies with my ex had overlapped in time. I imagined that Rare C'arter and Arty Sandra could possibly call each other sluts.

I wanted to do this not because I had that much active vengeance left in me—my capacity for that was almost as diminished as my appetite for food. I just wanted to do something that would serve as a funeral for my partnership. I wanted to bury it.

Another, more expedient marriage burial rite revealed itself. I was still logged in to the ex's account and able to hijack her status. I wrote 'I am a Dirty Pigfucker who enjoyed both actual sex and guilty internet sex in my shed while my ex-girlfriend Helen toiled in a low-prestige job she hates.'

It was over. So over. Facebook over.

The status disappeared almost immediately, as I was confident that it would. Recently she had been as fast with Facebook as she had long been with her beer. It was gone. Then, my phone sounded from the pile of stinking bones. I knew it was her. I just let it go. I couldn't exhume it.

I do know that I behaved like a stinking lunatic. The evidence of my stinking lunacy, which I would soon write all over the social internet, abides, and I was even somewhat aware that I belonged in a hospital for the freshly deceived. I knew that my ex was entitled to leave me. I knew that I had made it unpleasant for her to stay. I knew that I had been rotten in the past and that in the present I had little control over my libido or my foul tongue, and that poring over her correspondence looking for 'clues' was the work of an utter nut-loaf who'd been rising in a hate-oven for some time.

But I did stop looking so closely at the corpse of our marriage that third day. I knew that however hard I looked and whatever 'proof' I continued to find about the nature of this homicide, it was me who would remain a bloody crime scene.

'You can't solve a case whose probable location is you,' I wrote in a text to Celine.

Celine: OMFG, are you a divorcée or a really bad episode of CSI?

Helen: LIFE IS A HATE CAKE MADE OF LIES.

THE HELEN 100

I unwrapped the ruins of the chicken, but ate none. For an hour I lay with the cat, who did eat. All was deferred as I sobbed, just once, for the death of my blue nightdress and the theft of my nonsense name, just in time for the dolphin.

10

Forty-eight hours and two deceits since she left
Eleni, who was now making a big show of blowing on the wax to cool it before it entered my anus, said that I smelled of chicken. I said that this was unsurprising, but refused to elaborate. '*Why* do you smell of chicken on your hair, hands and dolphin-gina?'

I reminded Eleni that *she* had just told *me* words were hopeless, so I was doing everything I could to avoid using them. A vow that lasted just until this arrived:

> **Anticathexis:** I didn't really pull my weight on that last message and for this I can only apologise and roundly blame the weather or the lure of its antidote, St Kilda beach. I fear that I have let things pause uncomfortably.

Perhaps, to resume, we could just have a meta-conversation as the young people do, but I'm not really sure what that is and what it might involve. Um, hot innit? J Winking smiling face, perhaps with some animation.

Oh!

MidLifeISIS: A meta-conversation? Is that when our conversation has as its central topic the fact of our conversation? Plainly, I'm not sure what it is, either. But I have recently learned that words uttered for their own sake can be dangerous and that conversation that is too self-reflexive quickly kills promise. How do these things usually proceed, otherwise? Do we talk? I'm new here. It is warm. However, I am currently enjoying an evaporative cooler. This is a very efficient system.

With my dolphin turned up and towards the goddess Eleni, my thumbs shoved the screen at speed. It is difficult to exchange suggestive witty thoughts about the weather when you have access to neither paragraph breaks nor pants. However, I continued:

MidLifeISIS: I trust the beach provided some partial relief. Mildly smug emoticon, wearing sunglasses.

Anticathexis: Helen, the beach was not especially refreshing and nor was the sunburn I found there. I fear the chief benefit was an hour spent in an air-conditioned vehicle. I hope your efficient, evaporative AC was effective in cooling you down. Is it a bit creepy for a guy to go to the beach by himself? I wasn't there long as I had to leave my keys unattended while swimming. It remains so extraordinarily hot.

'Hot,' I said, and Eleni asked me why I looked so happy.

'Was it good news?' she asked.

'Shh,' I said, as she knows I know and like her sufficiently well to permit such rudeness.

MidLifeISIS: John. Of course it is unacceptable for a solitary man to spend even a moment at the beach. Unless, of course, he has a surfboard, a metal detector or a warrant to arrest a man alone at the beach. I am surprised you find it necessary to ask. After no more than four hours' experience with 'online dating', I have already lost faith in an algorithm that describes you as 'well mannered'.

MidLifeISIS: Oh. And. Evaporative cooling worked as efficiently as it always does in our dry climate and I was not much troubled by the heat. Thank you for your query and for the opportunity to describe the fascinating events of my go-go day.

I no longer felt the pain of waxing. Actually, I was no longer being waxed. Eleni had moved on to a complimentary head massage.

Anticathexis: 'Well mannered'? Don't blame the algorithm: garbage in, garbage out.

I tried to come up with a database-themed gag, but returned little. Probably because my head now felt so good.

MidLifeISIS: I got nothing. No function jokes from me. Frowny face. Perhaps we ought to have continued discussing the relative merits of refrigerant vs. evaporative air-cooling?

Anticathexis: Yes, let's do. I don't have algorithm jokes either and I refuse* to use a search engine to support this conversation—a restriction that also limits my capacity to talk about the relative merits of different types of air conditioning. I can talk about the absence of air conditioning, but where does that get anyone? Forward, without the luxury of paragraphs, I proceed. I imagine today you are enjoying your evaporative system, watching the cricket with a couple of tinnies in a vintage Australian World Series outfit circa 1983 (despite the fact it's a Test Match). I'm obviously doing the same, but without the AC. Aussie! Aussie! Aussie! P.S. You asked how these

> conversations generally proceed and I answer that this is contingent on a range of factors, although a general fade-out of quality and quantity of messages may be the most usual mode. I've been told that quite a few females here have been messaged by someone who wants to lick their feet. Has this happened to you yet? *Refusal is based on a passing whim and is in no way binding.

This was the stuff. This was hard fucking stuff. If C'arter's messages had been the ex's black tar, then those produced by this John person were my China white.

When manufactured with care, words *can* kill the pain of depilation and divorce for a bit. These were words handmade for me and, if we don't count Eleni's labour on my long untended person, they were the most generous opiate that had been given to me in years.

> **Public Service Announcement:** When seeking attachment via internet after being dumped again and again in the shitter, do try not to go bonkers for the very first person you meet who bothers to use a comma and dislikes your least favourite band.

Of course, perhaps Johns are not so very rare. Perhaps there are plenty of quite clever people on the internet adept at customising jokes about your local weather forecast. But I did not know if this was the case and, even if I did, I would not have found this funny person, who apparently did not look like a Wookie, any less intoxicating. He was the first person since she left to really write for me. He was the first who cared enough to regularly punctuate. Even with an em dash. Which isn't easy on an iPhone.

'Are you going to meet him?' said Eleni.

'Meet whom? I really have no notion of your meaning, young lady. Also, I think I can feel an unsightly hair remaining on my dolphin.'

Eleni, whose waxing is invariably seek-and-destroy, said that she had left no hair unpunished and reminded me that not only was I fairly crap when it came to concealing my emotions, but that I, being blind to a medical definition, had set my phone font to Very Extra Large. For the hour I had believed myself to inhabit a private potboiler, trading smut about the weather just like Lana Turner and John Garfield before they murder that unwanted husband in the heat, Eleni had been reading from over my dolphin.

'No, I will never meet him. I would like him to remain only a collection of funny words.'

'Look,' said Eleni. 'He's not that funny. But, even if he were, the point is, you spend too much time talking and writing words. Probably, this anti-whatever-it-is does, too. Your hoo-hoo is waxed and your nails are done, and if you put some make-up on you won't look so tired. So go and meet him with your new manicure. There's a good chance he'll like the colour. Which is "Lava", by the way. And beautiful. Not that you even care. It looks like he spends as much time typing in commas and things as you. You'll be, what's the word, copacetic. Simpatico. Whatever. And if you are, that's good for me, because you'll start coming back to the salon every week. Which will make me richer and you not so crazy with words. Live your life. Live your break-up, Helen. Don't write it.'

I told Eleni again that I had no intention of meeting anyone for whom I had already developed such an inimical passion. And then I explained I was booked for the night with a slab of Big Slavic Cock.

'Date anti-cantaloupe, catheter, or whatever he is called,' said Eleni. 'Then date the big dick Russian. Date the sleepwear lady. The chicken man. Date everyone. It's better than drinking or crying. Date them all. I dare you to go on one hundred dates. Now, give me some of your money.'

11

Forty-nine hours and one hundred stupid ideas since she left

Right. The matter of my survival was settled. I would go on one hundred dates. I would do so within the year. That would become the plan. And if it seems a little rash or capricious, well, yes, it was.

If you have not been horribly dumped, you may consider it unwise to base a plan on the self-interest of a beauty therapist who has just attacked your arsehole. If you have been horribly dumped, you may consider it unwise *not* to do so.

Maddie called as she said she would, and I gave her my one hundred news.

'Why the hell not?' she said. 'You should blog about it.'

As advice to enhance one's Online Brand, this was very sound—people might even *like* to read about someone else's

Whacky Dating Mistakes. As a route back to mental health, however, it was terrible. The best, and the most achievable, course of action was to keep things, for the moment, to myself.

There were a number of other reasons to not publish, chief among them that writing for an audience, even of consumers of discount beauty services, so often determined my emotional fate. I became what I wrote, and had never been able to write what I wanted to become.

Further, having been so recently the subject of unwanted surveillance, I needed a period of privacy.

I know there is a view that it is 'empowering' to celebrate and share one's imperfections broadly and perhaps, on occasion, this holds true. I am certain, for example, that the many women who post empowering naked pictures of themselves on Facebook feel thrilled by their moment of control. But I just wanted to stare at my own imperfect image for a while and learn, if not to affirm it, to actually tolerate those parts of it that I could.

Finally, I *had* already tried to write down an account of my condition for others to read. This was all I had:

> This year, I received a bag of expired dicks for Christmas and a colander of cold sick in time for New Year.

Which does not a moving first-person narrative make. My whining was so thin and unforgivable even I knew to throw it in the bin.

The only writing for which I upheld any talent or enthusiasm at all was direct correspondence. This faculty was of no interest to RedHot, who I would meet in a little over two hours. I should have been checking my closet to see if it contained anything that wasn't elasticised to wear in front of this apparently real man. Instead, I checked on messages from the phantom, John.

There were none. So I answered his latest:

MidLifeISIS: Foot licking? I have not yet been treated to such an invitation. I have, however, been offered the use of many, many penises yet to see their 20th birthday. It's very disappointing, to be candid, and you are, to date, the only identity for which I would not recommend some sort of urgent psychiatric or after-school care. Anyhow. Should we talk on the telephone or do we exchange messages for some time in the hope a mild limerence develops? Thank you, in any case. You have made me laugh at least once.

Mild limerence. *One* laugh. *Would not recommend* a psychiatrist. Way to underplay this hot commodity's intrinsic value. Actually, I had already visualised our wedding. Which would take place in a factory but would not, due to (a) my queer and Marxist politics and (b) my refusal to meet this man, in reality take place at all. Still. I was suddenly thin and it seemed a great shame not to make this known to many people who would marvel how I could pull off a white dress at my age.

This was limerence. Which could not, by the terms of its particular definition, ever be anything like 'mild'. I had misused this word as badly as I had misused my clitoris in recent days. Heavens, but I may have been quite close to rubbing the thing clean off.

Anticathexis: Limerence. Well. My rash Google embargo is over. 'Limerence is romantic infatuation that produces unusually obsessive fantasy.' I'm not really sure how limerence develops through the medium of text alone, although it does happen occasionally, I'm told. Sorry your online dating experience has been so disappointing. This place can tend to be the toilet for floating anonymous turds. Its low, low price of absolutely nothing also means that people tend to treat it as a chat room rather than an instrument by which contact can be made with a real person.

Oh! Oh. But did he mean that *he* was also using this place as a chat room? I mean, clearly I was using this place as a chat room where he was concerned. I had no intention then to ever meet him and interrupt the pleasure of his text, notwithstanding my coy reference to a conversation by telephone. But it seemed vital that he believed that this was my intention and vital, of course, that I in contrast could believe in his intention to meet me. Vital if the *mild* limerence were to develop.

Which I knew it had in text. And not at all *mildly*.

THE HELEN 100

I began to compose a reply, and was looking for how to spell and use the word 'propinquity' like a grown-up when a message from Maddie appeared on my phone.

'Close the app and open your closet,' she wrote. 'It's time to get dressed for date number one.'

12

Fifty hours and three chickens

I opened the closet, and the smell of her surged out.

Then, this very physical sensation of loss was disturbed, when I heard her keys in the door. But I didn't hear the person I felt that I had lost; she had in that short space of time become something very different. The stubborn stain of her in my memory, which had not, even for a second of internet chat, dissolved, bore only scant relation to the reality that was now moving through the house.

Of course, she hadn't really changed. The only thing that had changed was her inability to tolerate our life together. Still, this person appeared, as I understand such a person does to dumped people, as though a shady surgeon had opened the head, removed the brain and replaced it with a clockwork devil.

No one will ever be more of a stranger to you than your departed love.

Here she was, she said grimly, to pick up some of her things. And she was a pack-rat who had *so* many things, and she wanted to bring them to a place where she and they could 'grow'.

It had occurred to me to break or burn many of these things. But as I am less vengeful than I am lazy, I had destroyed only one. This was the 'assemblage' on which she had 'collaborated' with Sandra, winsome mother-of-two. It was a bracing multimedia piece I liked to call *You Fucked My Wife In The Shed So I Broke It*.

She started banging on about creative expression and freedom and the like, and then she mentioned the Facebook hacking business.

'You were spying on me,' she said.

'You were spying on me,' I said.

It was stale and ugly. I really couldn't bear either of us.

I thought about who I might call to divert me from the shit person I allowed myself to become with her, and I could only think of the barbecue-chicken man. He said he'd pop over with a tasty chook for a tasty etc. just as soon as he could.

I took Eleven, just in case she tried to catnap him, and locked both of us in the bathroom. I waited for the chicken man.

'You buy a lot of chickens,' he said when he promptly arrived.

'Yes, I do. Do you have a points program so I could get the occasional free bird?'

He had said that he didn't but that this was a fine idea.

'I should call it Frequent Flyer,' he said of my suggestion. Being quite preoccupied, I did not remind him that chickens, like most animals suitable for profitable slaughter, were not often known to fly.

A chicken myself, I had not yet set any rules for the ex. I ought to have made a date by which she must clear her gingivitis from the house. I ought to have asked for her keys. But I held myself back for a couple of reasons.

First, I believed, as most fresh garbage does, that I hadn't really been tossed. I told myself I didn't even *want* to be retrieved—not by that unfamiliar devil that would only take my soul back to clockwork hell. But I didn't quite believe she wouldn't try. (Truly believing in one's status as rubbish takes time.)

Second, here she was clearly having a relapse. She didn't come right out and tell me that if I was to shout and throw things, as is the usual entitlement of a divorcée, her condition would worsen, that her legs would stop working altogether, that the pain in her trigeminal nerve would leave her flat for a week. But, by now, she didn't need to.

She was pretty sick, my ex. Not cancer, but one of the other big illnesses that would begin with slow paralysis and end in premature death. For five years now, she had faced not only the palpable decline of her central nervous system but also the indignity of a diagnosis to which 'Awareness' ribbons are so routinely applied.

When things were cool in her world, she tended to remit. When they hotted up, so did the sheath around her nerves. I knew that stress enflamed her lesions; even the neurologist had said so. Hot weather. Heated conversation. People with infectious fevers. All these things were to be avoided.

It was, I think, an El Niño January. It was very hot and she was possibly a bit drunk. She'd left our breezy home for the unventilated attic of an old boyfriend; a chap with dreadlocks, a longstanding commitment to veganism and one of the frailest tempers you could hope to find this side of La Scala. With him, she would have little to eat, no place for peace and scant respite from the sun. All of which is to say she was now very shaky on her legs and the plaques inside her body needed no further heat from me.

I tried to hush. I crammed some chicken into my unmanageable gob.

Okay. I've now divulged that she was very ill and, in so doing, that I am an uncaring tit. You are at your liberty to loathe me and wonder that I could hack the Facebook account of a crippled lady. Or that I could not more easily forgive her incapacity and her infidelity and her moods. Or that I had told her, as I did now, that the things she had written to C'arter and Sandra were embarrassing shit.

I never did claim to be a tolerable human. I never did say that I was good. I only said that I was wounded.

Here she, or someone like her, was in the house. Here she was, telling me that she needed money and she truly hoped we could still be friends. Then she was screaming at me that I was a fascist when I told her that I had quit my job. A real, controlling, fascist bitch.

Here she was, sorting through her file of all the essays she had ever written in high school and smiling. I could not face her love for her own former efforts when she now didn't love me at all.

Christ. Why was she looking for yesterday's splendour when she hadn't even bothered to pack her immune-modulators for today? Did she need me to give her the injection? Oh, fuck her. Let her plaques flare up.

It was all fucking awful. I liked myself every bit as much as I liked the 'assemblage'. Which is to say, I held myself in no esteem at all, I felt a great surge of revulsion for the thing. I wanted to break it and myself.

We were *both* pathetic, most evidently when together. But especially me.

I'm telling you this as clearly as I can: there are reasons that she needed to be away from a prick like me. This is not a double-bluff. I damaged her work. I picked her apart. I did not hide my revulsion.

I locked myself away from her in the bathroom again and fed Eleven a small part of the chicken. I knew that this grief chicken must be our last. I was powerless to stop the weeping, the masturbation, the weeping masturbation and the pain, but I knew I could resist the chicken. I accepted a final chicken and I never became Frequent Flyer cardholder Number One.

As I looked at the cadaver of my indulgence, it occurred to me that, about to begin the first of one hundred dates, I now had a private customer loyalty program of my own. Of course I would be the sole administrator and the first and only member, and the reward would not be chicken but love. Or, if not love, then a life not so lacking in intimate supervision that I would again carelessly coat my cat or my twat in chicken grease.

For points, I would collect people instead of chickens. I would take myself on one hundred dates, as Eleni had advised as she plucked me. I would meet persons believing that one of them might love me and I might love them back. And I could even *tell* all of them about the formal nature of my project. Why not? If I told them 'This is date twenty-seven of one hundred', it might be cause for conversation and stop me from droning on about Karl Marx and/or my terrible break-up.

She was in the next room fondling her past. I was in bed with the grief-chicken making calculations for my future.

By my oily reckoning, the average number of more-or-less suitable love objects a person generally meets in a Western lifetime before a mutual declaration of love is made must be around, say, fifteen. I reasoned that I could easily exceed this figure in quite a short period. A year. After all, I was unencumbered by (a) gender preference (b) dignity and, having newly told my line manager to go and fuck herself with a concrete dildo, (c) regular employment. So I certainly had the time, if not the money, to date my way to the possibility of reward.

If I was sure to be polite and plainly disclose in advance my intentions, I would be loving and chosen.

It was January the Somethingth: I would need around two dates a week derived from internet profiles, existing friendship networks and, perhaps, the home-delivery food community.

She shouted again that she needed money. I called out to her, 'Sorry, no money. I'm broke.' Because I was.

She said, 'I have called my representative about that and she says you are legally obliged to offer me financial support.'

Familiar with her incapacity to use the phone for any purpose beyond immediate pleasure, I said, 'So Boozy Jo's Instant Hooch Delivery is dabbling in family law these days, is it?'

She said, 'Fuck off,' and knowing that her dad was able and willing to offer her money, I felt free to return this tribute through the bathroom door.

I wrote down some Terms and Conditions for the scheme:

1. If **Helen** fails to meet someone who can love her within a year, then her reward will be never having to bother loving anyone again. She will commit to a life of pleasant solitude.
2. If **Helen** does not fail, then she will be loved. And she will love. And, no, **Helen** doesn't think of love as the antidote to all her appalling poison. She simply *has* excess love and

prefers somewhere to store it. She is a fool for love. There is little for **Helen** to achieve in making any contrary claim. Is there, **Helen**?
3. **Helen** will attend one hundred dates in a year. Each of these dates will constitute a single point, but a maximum of five dates with a single suitor is permitted before points cease accumulation and/or someone calls the wedding caterers.
4. **Helen** may stop dating if she finds love, but not before.

The thought of one hundred dates was exhilarating. And then, as I noted the likelihood I would be late for my very first one, exhausting.

On the tram, I decided to lighten the load and count Eleni, who I would likely fail to charm but who had just touched my anus nonetheless, and then hard_4_ewe, because certainly, somewhere in world history such frank discussion about fucking someone in a merino costume had meant that you are married. I would also count the chicken man for his role as inspiration.

I took the decision to have ninety-seven more dates in what remained of the year. I gave it a name on my computer. I called it the Helen One Hundred and I texted its absurd details for Celine's approval. I knew she would be impartial in all her judgements, save for those where fashion was concerned.

Celine: Sure, why not? I can think of stupider things to do with a life. For example, I just bought a purple anorak from the internet, whose cruel lies about fashion I believed.

Helen: This is serious. I'm asking for advice.

Celine: A purple anorak.

Helen: You see a lot of shrinks. Can't you give me a psychiatric opinion?

Celine: Purple.

Helen: I need to know if you see any value in this plan?

Celine: Anorak.

Helen: I hate your selfish generation.

It was a peculiar promise to make to myself and I am still not entirely sure why it was made. I guess I just needed some clear guidelines. Where else but to an organised insanity does someone who has lost love turn? Hm?

By now the ex had left, with perhaps one fiftieth of her belongings. I returned to final thoughts of my plan.

Availability was my only condition for a date, and so it remained. I would eventually draw the line at suitors who were younger than hard_4_ewe, who I had learned was 29, or older than my dad, who was seventy-three. I would make some adjustments to a project that Ameera would generously call 'quixotic' and my neighbour Dahlia, the street's best gardener, 'a mad woman's laundry'. That Celine would repeatedly describe as 'not as stupid as a purple anorak'.

It was, of course, fairly stupid, and I would fall into days of compunction. But I would not stop until I found someone.

*

You who are newly dumped may find my account instructive. Then again, you may prefer to sit alone and think. And, yes, this might be good advice for those ten people in all of earth's sad history who were able to (a) think or (b) be alone in the months following invasion of their heart by a pod of angry dolphins. But I needed some fucking supervision.

You may, quite sensibly, decide to go to Tuscany instead. You may elect to ignore the mild advice at the core of this absurd text, which is that we who are grieving for the loss of a partner and/or our own goodness must do something differently.

13

Fifty-one hours, one date

RedHot, who was actually called Anton, was not an especially disappointing man. He was cheerful and reasonably bright. He was handsome, too, after a Putin sans-the-psychosis-but-with-the-hair type of fashion. He had a good, strong nose and a slim accent so that when he pronounced the mild 'e's and the final 'n' of my name, they sounded agreeably brutal. 'Hiyalun-n.' It was Hollywood KGB.

He was untroubled by my faithful fifteen minutes of lateness, a facility I admire. Anton was, in fact, perfectly fair. His choice to play me an iPhone slideshow of his nine-year-old's triumphs at physie, however, did seem a poor one. Particularly when we consider he had offered me, just hours before, 'a ride on his Big Slavic Cock'.

Obviously, a 'ride' on a 'cock' of any provenance or size was something I had actively sought on the internet and this offer did not come *ex nihilo*. But the display of a pre-teen girl on a pommel horse really did. God, this was a terrible surprise.

'Look at my adorable daughter!'

Fuck, no.

He served up her image no fewer than three minutes into a meeting and yet to suffer a silence so intolerable, it could only be filled with a girl. I found the portraits depicting his child's physical virtue more shocking than any of the dick pics I had seen in recent days.

I had not before that evening ever knowingly entertained the thought of sex with someone's father, so this moment was, for me, unexpected. But Anton had introduced it naturally.

It was clear then he was not a man given to socially inappropriate behaviour. Within the very standard inappropriateness of internet-sex chat, reference to his Big Slavic Cock had been perfectly okay. And even correctly spelled. His greeting, too, had been fine, if not a little chaste. He had leaned in to kiss me less like the cowboy capitalist Red Hot Russian I had been promised by internet message and more like a Cold War functionary.

Still, sub-zero Apparatchik snuggles aside, he seemed an equable, affable person. And sane, other than for the fact he was showing me pictures of his daughter in a ludicrous lilac leotard.

It began to occur to me that it was not unusual but quite standard for male persons of my age in my era to boast, or to complain about their children, even, and perhaps especially, in the prelude to sex.

I wondered if we would have sex surrounded by stuffed toys and family photos. I wondered if I met other men of Anton's age, sex might be rescheduled altogether 'because my little man needs me at his soccer game'. And that I might be expected to consider the terms of such delay super, super hot.

Were childcare considerations now a form of foreplay when uttered by men? If so, would that privilege of turning parental hardship into desirability also be extended to the many persons of my gender who face so much trouble finding a reliable babysitter? Or could it even soon be possible for me to say, 'I'll be a little late as I need to express Eleven's anal gland,' and know that these words of responsible cat-parenting also provoked desire?

Sheesh. Some people do find themselves adorable for no good reason at all.

Actually, I didn't think Anton was such a deluded tool. He seemed rationally confident. And, like all rationally confident people, would not be easily given to offence. So I surmised it would be fine to ask him why in blazes I was looking at a picture of his daughter in her leotard.

'Do you often display pictures of your daughter on internet sex dates?' I said.

'Yeah, why not. Honestly, most chicks go for it.'

If I learned anything new that day about my generation of fathers, it is that many people find such paternal devotion delightful. Most being the fathers themselves.

To be clear, I see no fault with emerging masculine interest in after-school activities and it's really just marvellous that the man of the present is taking his Big Slavic Cock out of traditional parenting roles and into physie, soccer, amateur productions of *Pippin*, etc. Who says you can't be both responsible for half-time snacks and completely down to fuck? But I did think I would prefer not to climax in a bedroom decorated with finger-paintings.

Frankly, the vacant art of children gives me the heebie-jeebies. I certainly didn't want it anywhere near a cock, of the Big Slavic kind, or any other.

I identified Single Sex Daddy as a dominant erotic style among my peers. In fact, I *had* noticed preliminary evidence of this often on my run through the park. I had watched divorced and demonstrably fertile men between thirty-five and forty-five stand in groups by the sandpit. I saw them faux-casually lift the hems of their high-end skatewear sweaters to scratch rock-hard abs with supple hands and I heard them say things to each other like, 'Yeah, Bra. I'm going to feed my little guy some smashed av for lunch!' within earshot of the well-to-do mothers. As though somehow gently pulping a soft fruit and feeding it to a child were acts of such uncompromised masculine intensity, their report would make her whip off the Stella McCartney compression pants and beg him to do her hard in the shitter.

As it turned out, she was rarely unconquered. The pants came off, as Stella had perhaps intended. *Most chicks go for it*. Yes, I am certain that they do. Anton was simply playing the odds. But he needn't have. I was completely down to fuck. Mildly less so as I struggled to abolish the vision of a child from what I still regarded as a most inappropriate context.

The pub where we had met was so unadorned it looked to be designed by a Methodist property developer. One that more generally dabbled in those hideous, shiny 'city living' apartments built to contain an army of divorced, av-smashing men who paraded their spawn on weekends in the hunt for good park pussy. This architecture did not so much spring from an actual style school as it did from the reluctance to engage its occupants, thereby minimising the possibility they would note its fundamentally impractical materials. It was chiefly mirrors, without even the smoke.

There were very few patrons and a lot of polished surfaces that shone bright. I wondered if Anton had chosen this bare reflective place so he wouldn't be seen with me by anyone much but both of us at several angles. I decided that I didn't care and started to worry that the glare had compromised my look. I had followed a make-up tutorial from the internet that Celine had sent. I had shaded the folds of the lids of my flagging, red eyes and coloured their corners with white pigment which, cosmetic wisdom has it, distracts from the ravages of misery. I had also brushed at least 10 per cent of the cat hair from my dress.

I looked good. Possibly good enough for harsh lighting. The dress was a form-fitting khaki thing that I hadn't wriggled into since the nineties; a dress old enough that it had long ceased to be conspicuously undesirable. Which is the impression I also wished to make myself.

I caught sight of the dress in one of the pub's foofety thousand mirrors and saw that the back of it would have showed my newly compact arse to marvellous advantage had it not been coated in, what's that, kitty litter. Not just speckled, but actually coated. With bits in.

I couldn't be certain how or when this filth had joined itself to my frock, and I wasn't going to examine it or any one of its faecal bits to assess the area. But I did note that much of the grime was a greyish hue, which meant that it was made from bentonite clay. This was a material my ex and I had always tended to shun in favour of more specialty environmental fare and which one of us only ever bought from the local shop when normal routine was suspended. Such as when one of us dumped the other for good. Which is to say, this was some pretty fresh shit laid in kitty litter, which somehow felt worse to wear than old shit.

Oh. I remembered. Dropping the garment on the laundry floor as I looked about, of all things, for stain remover to rub a spot of virtually nothing from its bib. This was some farm fresh artisanal shit.

Giddy from internet chatter and the dishonest, unhelpful advice that I was 'effortlessly stunning', I had expended no effort at all on an entire half of my person. In the front, I looked reasonable. Possibly even attractive. To the rear, we saw an early expressionist work by the back end of Jackson Pollack's most outrageous cat.

There was no hiding the foul grime at all. I could run, which would reveal the very fresh mess quite fully to Anton, and then to everyone on the tram home. Or I could just sit there and hope that Anton couldn't smell it, which I believed that I now could, and might mistake it for fashion-forward appliqué. Or I could have a glass of alcohol. Which I had not in nearly two years.

'Drink?' said Anton.

Intravenously. Please.

I had promised myself not to ask Anton the Russian about the last days of impure Marxist-Leninism, through which he had said that he had lived. This was a vow broken due to a number of influences.

First, if I were more offensive than the cat poo on my dress, maybe he wouldn't notice the cat poo on my dress. Second, I was completely trolleyed halfway into a single beer. Third, he started it.

Of course, my normal conversation, even on a day when the shit show goes dark, is lacking in measure. I fight the urge to contradict persons, even those with whom I agree. I believe this is not so much the result of a deep personal flaw but just a bad habit, like travelling to India for the 'wisdom'. I do it often and I know this well, which is why I had prepared myself to avoid a potential clash of economic standpoints and had even asked Celine to text me the words 'Do not ask him about the Soviet experiment, you stupid purple anorak' by 6 p.m.

But Anton started talking about work at 5.58 p.m. Which is fine, of course, and if I had been engaged in work of any sort at the time, I might have also said something like, 'Work! It's all go go go!'

Work was, of course, less than slow after I had advised Brynlee to take her job to the arse doctor. As I had so little to say about my own working life, Anton made broad appraisal of his own in the IT business that he owned and he began to talk, as people do, about the failings of others.

'You just can't get good help,' he said.

It was just like pre-perestroika Russia, he went on. Kids today are just like that. Everyone he knew under Gorbachev just felt entitled. It's all Want Want Want and Me Me Me with these kids. They're the problem with this economy. Why do people have no hope or drive? Government handouts, that's why.

So he started it. He really did. A capitalist should not be surprised when he strips down his dreary ideology and a nearby communist finds the tease obscene.

I *did* make an effort and I did *not* point out that if his birth year was as he had claimed it on the internet, Anton would have been just twelve at the end of the Cold War and was, therefore, hardly qualified to hold forth with a firsthand account of entitled glasnost labourers. Ergo, he was either lying about (a) his age or (b) his experience of communism.

I didn't say it. Nor did I venture that the social and economic problems in a nativist Russia of the present made the problem of mere personal 'entitlement' seem like small potatoes. Can we really claim communism to be the colossal failure the West imagines while capitalist Russia stands unsteady today in crime and debt and sectarian hate, Anton? Can we really?

I didn't say these things, either. But I did eventually, in the face of a bit about The Workers of Today and Their Idle Ways, ask him if, perhaps, this was not the result of individual failure of people but the structural failure of capitalism. Which, by the by, was hardly doing much for social equity in our own nation. Where were all these handouts going, other than into the coffers of large corporations?

So he started it. To give me my due.

To give him his due, Anton tried to turn my socialist rambling to sexy advantage. Which wasn't easy. Trying for a sparky Rock and Doris dispute that would end when the argument faded into a tangle of hot love wasn't easy with me because I take myself very seriously.

'Workers just don't know how good they have it, blondie,' said Anton, whose coders had recently refused to code without the reward of overtime.

'This is the delusion of the merchant producing surplus capital at the expense of a labourer's mind and body,' said me.

'Oh. You're sparky! But people just don't try to better themselves these days. I did. That's why I have a lovely home in Balwyn. Perhaps you'd like to see it,' he said.

'This is the justified rage of the late-capitalist worker for whom the myth of the possibility of upward mobility has begun to fall away,' I said.

He then said something like, 'You're a feisty one, aren't you?' and I said, 'Fuck off with your patriarchal egotism.'

Unfair of me, really. Especially given that I had at least 50 per cent of my tits on display from a balconette bra and had done everything to appear like a woman who observed patriarchal standards. Which, really, for the sake of a Big Slavic Cock ride, I had wanted to be.

It's true that I was a little out of practice on that score, having been in an ostensibly monogamous and committed relationship with a woman who wore khakis. But it was less a lack of familiarity with straight convention—which is, in any case, ubiquitous and impossible for all females, homosexual or otherwise, to ignore—than the return of another bad habit that made me so tedious on this date: Herr Marx.

I shouldn't have chosen a former Soviet as my first date. It made it so much more likely that Karl would appear. Which he did, to kill the commodity of conversation.

I like conversation. I like to talk before and during sex and ask, 'Can I touch you there?' Laboured talk about consent is often good for me—perhaps this is because I once worked in the public service. Anyhow, I should have simply talked to Anton about where I could touch him and not quite so much about the accumulation of private wealth and the public pain that inevitably follows.

THE HELEN 100

For a spell, I refused Anton much opportunity to speak at all. He called me a 'spicy little pinko' and tried to respond, again and again, to my dreary chat with a spur of libidinal conflict. Meanwhile I kept repeating things from a volume I am not sure that I have ever really understood. Marx was about to rise up to end the possibility of sex. The workers of the world would not unite at Anton's well-appointed home in Balwyn.

There was a spectre haunting my vagina. It was the spectre of communism.

'Look,' he said. 'I think you're cute. But you really need to shut up.'

Which, of course, I needed to do then, and do rather generally, and while the weight of that knowledge rested on my vocal folds for just long enough for him to speak, he said, 'I'm sorry, but I have to take this,' and walked through the shiny, empty hall to talk to someone who probably knew how to talk.

Anticathexis: I trust that you are in finest fettle after the Australian cricket victory. For which we may all claim proud and total responsibility. I should say, to address your earlier question about the telephone, that I am not content with only written banter—however much I may appreciate exchange with clever and amusing persons like yourself. I do try to meet and speak with people if they seem interested. This is not particularly easy for me. I ought to confess that I'm rather awkward and shy,

> so meeting people gets me outside of a comfort zone, whose modest limits are most easily described by this disclosure: I'm a twitcher. I actually enjoy watching, and documenting, birds. I suppose it's wrong to use people here as some kind of personal therapy, but that's really just an externality—I actually do want the types of 'long-term relationship' or 'short-term relationship' that are selected in my profile. (Do you also want what you have declared? And what does the 'activity partner' box even mean? Is it a euphemism of some type? Is everyone aware of its truer meaning but me?)

John had returned, in explosively generous form, to my phone, even if Anton was still occupied with his. *If* Anton was occupied with his phone. Perhaps he had absconded to the playground and was now pulling off a willing mother's high-end compression pants. Perhaps he had alerted the authorities to the presence of a criminally tedious communist.

Whatever the case, I was tempted to remain here and mash my screen for John, whose bird-watching and bashfulness were glorious guarantees of a neurodevelopmental disorder. *Hot*. However, more pressing, I knew that I must make my way, backwards (insofar as such a preposition was possible in a hall full of mirrors) to the ladies' room and divest myself of cat shit.

Naturally, the loo in a sad palace like this was empty of nearly everything but surfaces. There was no paper towel, just two of those orange dialysis-looking dryers into which one inserts the hands. So I backed into a cubicle wall to which one of those frugal portion-controlled loo-paper dispensers was affixed. I spent some minutes gathering up dozens of the mean, tiny squares of frictionless paper, no single one of which was up to the job of cleaning even half of an Eleven turd, moistened them at the hand-basin, then shot back inside the cubicle when the door swung open.

As I dabbed at the crap and the clay, using my phone camera to see where I'd positioned the shiny paper in relation to the cat waste, I heard two female voices unite in their approval of a 'foreign hottie' who was, apparently, on his phone outside the pub entrance to his little Princess Anastasia.

'Ooh. I love a hot dad!' said one.

'It's so sexy how they look after their little ones!' said another.

I still didn't get the 'childcare is hot' thing. But, I didn't get quite a bit of the useful wisdom that appears to come so easily to others. E.g., basic makeup techniques, shutting the fuck up and dressing myself like a grownup in clean clothes. Or, not writing 'You must go on. I can't go on. I'll go on' on the lavatory wall.

I was a horrid animal. Clearly, this date failure was my failure and, in the case that Anton, who apparently *had* received a legitimate phone call and *had not* run off to report me to Joseph McCarthy/bend a yummy mummy over a seesaw to deliver Slavic cock, did return to the table, I determined to try to see the 'sexy' side of parenting as many other ladies plainly do.

Incredibly, Anton had returned.

'Welcome back, Karla Marx,' he said. 'Do you like the theatre?'

As it happens, I *do* quite like the theatre. Not all of it, but, obviously, as a tedious Marxist, Brecht. And some other plays that I had seen, and I had seen many at the time of a particularly endurable contract for a now-dead listings website which paid me to write very short reviews. I was no connoisseur, but when I was given a pair of tickets to see Ian McKellen as Lear in an RSC production, I knew that this was marvellous. Or it was marvellous right up until interval when the ex said that she had seen *enough*. So I never got to see Regan go batshit and take out Gloucester's eye.

I remembered how she could only ever be dragged to the theatre. Then I saw the possibility that I may be now *invited* to the theatre and I felt briefly but completely exhilarated.

Public Service Announcement: No matter how cruelly you have just been dumped in cat shit by your ex, you can expect a sensation of liberty to fill you with its welcome heat at some point. There is a glorious moment where you will feel free. It may come when you're standing at the refrigerator and begin to understand that you can now fill it with *anything* you fancy. It may come when you see that Netflix has added *The Shawshank Redemption* and you know you are not obliged to watch it now, or ever again. Or you may be in an icy Coldplay pub, more or less scrubbed of poop, and a creditably handsome man seems ready to ask you to join him for a play and you know you'll answer yes.

'Yes, Anton. I *do* like the theatre.'

And he asked if I would join him there that evening.

Well, YES, Sexy Dad. Sexy Oscar Wilde but Heterosexual Aesthete Sex Dad.

Take me at once to the stage!

*

I learned that night there are certain theatrical productions from which one should feel morally obliged to flee at half-time.

The call to Anton had been from the former Mrs RedHot who found herself unable to escort little Anna Karenina RedHot, of leotard repute, to an evening performance of *Barbie Live: The Musical*. Or, as I now prefer to know it, *Regan, Please Gouge Out Both My Eyes So That I Don't Have To Watch This Pigfuckery*.

The entertainment was, of course, a horror. Frankly, if I learn you have exposed your issue to this toxin, I am fucking calling the welfare people. And not just because you are filling your daughter's unconscious with glitter and her future with a self-loathing so intense that by twenty-five she will be living on a diet of diets and Xanax. It is because your kid's formative experience of camp is so low they will never grow to appreciate Sondheim or Fosse.

The photo slideshow was bad enough. But an enforced meeting with the little Pushkin Pants depicted at a kid's musical was completely out of order.

The child was a turd. I know this is a terrible thing to say about the eight-year-old product of divorce.

I'm absolutely sure, of course, that this turdiness wasn't Baby Bakunin's fault. Obviously she had vile parents who deemed *Barbie* not only suitable entertainment, but entertainment so significant that it could not be missed. Not even in the middle of an internet date with a virtual guarantee of rough sex. Which, I hoped, was exactly the activity that the ex Mrs RedHot was now enjoying, as the chances that I would decreased with every tainted tune brought to us by the licensees of Mattel. Please, let someone in the world, aside from my ex, be getting laid.

The problem with little Chekhov RedHot could really be seen up on stage.

It seemed that in an effort to erase her past as an impossibly proportioned idiot slut given to utterances like 'Math is hard!' and 'Let's go shopping!', Barbie's new authors had turned her into an 'empowering' figure. I rarely feel great about the delusion of freedom and I worry quite a bit when I see it served up to kids.

The lie of empowerment was Anna Pavlova's problem. Christ, it was nearly everyone's problem, including mine, if

Facebook, with all its empowered selfies, or if contemporary workplaces, with their invitations to Be The Best Helen You Can Be, were any reliable guide.

False empowerment was one of the big problems of the age. All the fucking awful songs were about fucking self-esteem. My least favourite of which was called 'Finally My Moment to Shine'. This bore no little resemblance to the company song selected by the Daily Deals office, which was possibly by Taylor Swift. Who is, I am encouraged to believe, totally empowered as a woman.

Led by the arrant stupidity of what popularly passes as empowering feminism, Barbie's function was now to make little girls Feel Good About Themselves by offering the advice that you should 'be brave and be strong and just be yourself!' Which is all well and good, but utterly gainsaid when done in a series of costumes all designed by a certifiable misogynist on the back of a plastic pink pony.

And if this glitzy loop of visual faux-affirmation were not enough, all of the characters in this pussy pageant reminded their young audience that the greatest work of girls is to be seen.

Barbie had apparently become some sort of multi-platform celebrity mentor for the 'play'. Much of the 'plot' seemed to involve her showing other girls how to *sparkle sparkle sparkle* in front of the world's waiting cameras.

Personally, I preferred Barbie's early work. It was better when she just mumbled about how much she hated mathematics.

I had felt uncomfortable seeing the pictures of Bubba Baryshnikov in her physie outfit and fairy outfit and various Future Slut outfits, and not just because it seemed wrong to think about children within an hour of having rough sex on a playset near a pleasant home in Balwyn. But now I was faced with this whole rotten over-supply of illusory self-esteem Anton was clearly inculcating in his daughter.

I had worried that this little girl was being raised to believe that her image was also the register of her value. How could she not, with so many images held by a father with whom she no longer lived? He didn't have her in his home. Just her images. I worried that the poor little turd would shortly go on to star in a short film with a title like *Co-ed Sluts Volume 17* and neglect all of her promise in the growing sport of aerobic dance in favour of documented face baths.

(*Not* that there's anything wrong with a face bath. Or for the payment or receipt of a face bath for the purposes of pornographic film. Still, I didn't imagine little Kropotkin would go on to be one of those truly 'empowered' stars of adult cinema, who do, I know, actually exist. She'd be one of those porn stars less fortunate. Another exploited labourer living in the service of the image and the lumpen-wang.)

These thoughts may be attributed to the fact that I am a pessimistic arsehole who hates joy. But I do not believe that I conspired to kill it as the RedHot family did, or those awful Barbie people with all their faux empowerment. You think *I'm* negative? You don't *know* negative until you've seen *Barbie Live: The Musical.*

You think 'government handouts' are destroying the Kids of Today, Anton? You think the state honouring its contract to its citizens is going to fuck people up? When we're sitting here with your already imprisoned daughter being led to believe that 'feeling beautiful' will set her fucking free? As though 'feeling beautiful' were some hard-won human right, up there with free assembly and democratic elections. As though being looked at were always a joy and never a yoke.

I wasn't feeling super sexy anymore. And I certainly did not want to be looked at.

Still, I didn't really mind that much that Anton, staring straight ahead, sitting between me and Gorky, now had a fistful of my tits. Groping is not looking.

Possibly, the near-naked eighteen-year-olds on stage—who had now begun to recite some dialogue about a 'magic blue crystal', which made me think of Tuco Salamanca, the sociopathically violent blue meth salesman from *Breaking Bad*—had aroused him and he was just grabbing my left mam simply because it was there. I didn't care. Anything to deliver me from this pink mouth of hell.

I wasn't getting laid tonight. My vagina had fused shut like Barbie's. With Anton's hand now halfway up my skirt, searching for a waxed plastic mound, I picked up my phone and tried to write my way out of that place.

MidLifeISIS: Thanks for your candour, John. In my own case, 'activity partner' is certainly a euphemism. Which is to say, if there were the option 'Jizz Bucket', I would have checked that one without pause. In short, I am seeking only one or several enthusiastic sexual encounters before such time as my tits go south. If this is of no interest to you, a seeker of the more serious long- or short-term, I understand utterly and thank you so much for your time. If, however, it *is* of interest to you, I thank you in advance for your cock.

Barbie was asking the audience of little girls what they aspired to be when they grew. 'Jizz bucket,' I muttered. And Vladimir RedHot screamed, with the rest of them, 'PRINCESS'.

'That's not a job description. You must learn to be more realistic,' I said. Audibly. And then Anton, who had not yet removed his hand from 'my most familiar part', looked at me with naked hatred.

'What? *What?*' I said.

'You can't shatter her dreams.'

Yeah. Well. You shattered mine about Big Slavic Cock, Comrade.

As the pleasure of judging poor parenting technique was the only one that night I was likely to find, I started on one of my bad speeches.

'Well, the plain fact is that Australia has only ever produced one actual princess. Given the ongoing historical trend to reject the vestiges of monarchy in Europe, I can bet there will be no more. Your daughter, little Joanne Stalin, should know this.

Also, you are Russian and so you must take a fairly gloomy view of what it means to be a princess. Shot or bludgeoned to death in the early twentieth century. Look, mate, I'm thinking about leaving because I've really had enough family-friendly entertainment.'

Now he withdrew his hand from my dead poonanny.

Anton said that he *too* had endured more than was sufficient to his liking and that I probably *should* leave before I so injured the self-esteem of his Russian nesting doll that he summoned theatre security and had me banned from children's musicals for life.

Comrade. *Dasvidaniya.*

14

Fifty-five hours and one night of paralysing empowerment

I was fairly cross as I made my way home on the No. 67 tram. I'd disbursed hundreds of dollars on painful beauty therapy and several unpleasant minutes in a toilet cubicle just to make myself presentable for the good, hard knocking I'd been explicitly promised but had never received.

I was now angry-horny instead of pathetic-horny, and I briefly considered the possibility of returning to the theatre and demanding that Anton finish his hand job lest I sue.

Instead, I calmed myself and reasoned that I had racked up not one but two dates for that evening. There had, after all, been both an extreme change of venue and of mood. Five date points, therefore, had been accrued by 9 p.m.

My phone was blinking.

> **Anticathexis:** Your candour is also appreciated. This is, naturally, of great interest to me, Jizz Bucket. Perhaps we should meet tonight to allow an assessment of our suitability for the object in question. John. Maniacally winking face, definitely with some animation.

What the fuck ever and, really, why not? I couldn't even remember one fifth of my elaborate writer's rationale for preferring not to meet this fairly funny, possibly handsome, and almost certainly on the autism spectrum fellow. Something or other to do with the fear that I would end up writing like E.L. James. A result, at least, which would have been more profitable, and even slightly less dull, than the interminable exchange of terrible messages on dating sites. Other, of course, than *these* messages with John, whose tempo and substance I continued to find analgesic, and which now held mild hope for profit. By which we mean cock.

> **MidLifeISIS:** Let's. I should probably stop saying 'cock' so much, though.

> **Anticathexis:** Do please let me know your thoughts on meeting this evening, then. Where and when? PS, say 'cock' as much as you like.

> **MidLifeISIS:** You should feel free to nominate a place and time, too. I am currently in the south-east without a

vehicle or a clue, and I am always grateful when someone else can make a decision. Oh, and I take it as read that our conversation and proximate meeting is not a matter for discussion by anyone but ourselves? Cock.

Anticathexis: Fully understand. Discretion on my part is assured. Am I correct in assuming a meeting venue should therefore be somewhere out of the public eye, or is that going a bit overboard? I might suggest Pause (sp?), but I've got a nagging suspicion there's some kind of zany spelling involved in the title, which may make it a difficult place for you to find. You may know a quiet nook closer to your place or we could meet in that big park on Glenferrie Road—I'll bring the generic flying disk; you bring the golden retriever.

MidLifeISIS: These all sound like decent plans. Make one and I'll be there. I am glad that this is an evening meeting as I am old and look much softer in crepuscular light.

I now understand that I was being a bit princessy in failing to accede to one of John's several considered suggestions. Perhaps I was tired. Perhaps I was not yet accustomed to choosing the place I'd like to be. Or perhaps Barbie's message of venal self-esteem had rubbed off on me. Make all my arrangements! It's Barbie's time to shine!

Anticathexis: Low light is similarly kind to my appearance so Pause (sp?) might be a suitable venue. As I may have mentioned earlier, there are no claims on my time tonight so whenever you like is fine by me. Perhaps a telephone call would be prudent?

I sent John my telephone number and he sent me his and I, in fairly unrelated news, began to decompose.

Both the events of the day and the possibility that the day may yet contain more events started to diminish my angry, horny spark. I was, being either forty-three or forty-one, averse to spending so many social hours away from home.

I recognised how far away home still was, and the prospect of enduring the nervous intimacy of public transport for another six stops drubbed me further. Then, when I recognised that home no longer really existed, I began to cry. Like a Barbie, at first: just tiny tears and a pint-size whimper, such as we might hear from a King Charles spaniel who has found an uncomfortable Kink in his luxury bed. Then, on the Glen Huntly Road, I cried much more like a bull-mastiff on a road in the last bloody moments of life. And I don't know why, but I suspect it had something to do with the beer. The one that I had earlier, and the one wrapped in brown paper being emptied by the man with the rusted fly zipper sitting opposite me on the tram.

I have tended for at least a decade to avoid drinking. If I'm not physically ill after two standard drinks then I have been drinking so gradually time has afflicted me with a guilt-tinged hangover. Either way, when I've had just one, my head is in my hands and I am suffering that chemical regret more typically brought to folks by the morning after. It is through this prism of immediate emotional and/or physical pain that I had come to understand viscerally, if not logically, drinking as an act of destruction.

I saw the man with a beer and it seemed he was quite unwell and that he did not have a home. I thought of the ex with a beer and an illness and now without a home. And I knew that neither of them was responsible for their pain, or for their entirely fathomable refusal to stare it down. Drink pauses pain.

I saw neither that she nor the man sitting opposite could just be 'empowered' by this straitjacket life with its rusted restraints and, fuck, I felt *so bad* for ever blaming her for anything at all. Including, and especially, the drink. Baby, I am sorry.

I am reluctant to describe my ex as an alcoholic, and not because she didn't drink like a fish. She had drunk like a school of especially thirsty mackerel. I am reluctant to call her an alcoholic because my drink-averse metabolism had come to disqualify me from such assessment, and so had my lack of pain.

Drink would often take my ex to the past. She would talk often about how good the vibe was in 1994, the days before kids ruined raves with their inappropriate twerking and, most troubling to me, the promise she had as a writer in school.

I have never understood nostalgia, especially for one's past exertions as a writer, which I frequently, and often not unreasonably, see as ridiculous just minutes after they are published or complete. I like nostalgia about as much as I like drinking.

But I might understand nostalgia, and drink, better if I had ever known real pain. It struck me that she had idealised her past because her past had not afflicted her with such physical pain. Once, before she met me, she didn't hurt.

Still crying at home, I called a woman I know named Kay. Kay was a recovering drunk, and I knew was in the sort of program where discretion was assured. I told her about the saddest days and nights of my ex's drinking. I said she was an alcoholic. And not because I felt an entitlement to do so but because I am awful, and because Kay had asked 'Was she an alcoholic?' as recovering addicts often will.

I could have said nothing, but instead I said, 'I think so,' before I could actually think so. Being sacked by a long-term spouse curses one with unthinking candour.

In an atmosphere of uncertainty and unstable truth, we can begin to believe that the truth will set us free. I had set the truth, or my version of it, free whenever I could for two days now, and it had returned to me to that night on the No. 67 tram.

Truth. Nostalgia. Drink. None of these things worked to pause my pain. So I just cried to the point where I thought I might need to call Gerard. Then I cried to the point where it started to be a bit funny.

I slept for an hour or two and woke when a hangover and a cat bore down on me. A hangover was always unwelcome. But this cat was always a pleasure. At some point in the ten years we had spent together, he had deduced that if he put a paw in just the right place on my bladder, I would wake. I never minded: I adored him and attributed even his most wilful behaviour to exceptional feline intelligence.

'E-le-ven!' I mock scolded him.

He butted my hand with his head then sniffed the place where the chicken had been. It was time to return this cat to his regular, strict and comically expensive program of eating. Although apparently it was not yet time for me to suffer any such restriction and I looked, as an undisciplined person does, at my phone for midnight notifications.

Public Service Announcement: Newly dumped persons should try to avoid sleeping with their phones within reach. Particularly if they find that they can ever sleep at all.

Hours before, John had texted:

Let's go for a walk in the park then. Are you familiar with the one I mentioned earlier? Does it meet the criterium?

Then, he had tried to call a few minutes later.

Then, in a fit of tender interest doubtless brought forth by my beguiling offer to function as his Jizz Bucket, he had texted again:

I can always do tomorrow. It's probably too late, and you may be sensibly reluctant to walk in a park in moonlight conditions with someone you've only just met online.

And once more:

Your response, or lack thereof, is completely justifiable. I suspect it might be down to the 'criterium' confusion of Greek with Latin in my earlier message. Which you may consider forgiving as my ambitious attempt to look more cleverer than I are.

Look, I thought he was pretty funny. And I needed a laugh, so I texted:

When you confused a bicycle race (criterium) for a standard that might govern a bicycle race (criterion), I would have blamed it on your phone's autocorrect if I were not myself, after recent receipt of many teens' mistyped messages, now internally set to autocorrect. I really didn't notice.

And just in case he was awake but sleepy, and so now was, as I *always* was, disposed to rip a phrase like 'I really didn't notice' from its contextual mooring and infer from it 'I couldn't give less of a fuck about a fuckstain like you', I texted, reassuringly:

And genuine apologies for the tardiness of reply. I shan't go into details, but let's just say that I spent the better part of the evening occupied with the care of an eight-year-old girl, and that the future for my gender looks as ordinary as its past.

He was awake:

I would have loved to have owned 'criterium', but I'm all about the honesty. Very ardently when there are no plausible alternatives available to me.

And:

There is no lyric in our familiar history of hits that fills me with as much fear as that, which warns that the children are our future. Sorry about the patriarchy.

I wrote:

Whitney, may she rest, knew that the greatest love of all was onanistic.

John: I know I learned to depend on me.

Helen: I'm depending on myself right now.

Yes, you may snigger that I told him I was 'bating. But, this was actually inevitable and therefore not my fault. Did you know that ninety-seven per cent of all associations that have their origin in an online dating service will produce conversational allusion to this act at some point between the exchange of one and fifty messages? I urge you to confirm this finding in the well-regarded work of reference, *Untruths I have Pulled From My Arse* by Dr* H. Razer (*Not a real Doctor).

John: Well. Convention now obliges that I ask: What are you wearing?

Helen: Apparently, the frock I left the house in.

John: Please describe it.

Helen: Honestly, it's covered in kitty litter and bits of shit.

John: Hot. SO hot. Well, finish yourself off, luv. I've blown.

John: Srs, though, What KIND of frock?

Helen: First, my ability to describe raiment in text has never, to my occasional professional frustration, been strong. Second, even if I were able to meaningfully evoke it as A-line or bias cut or as chartreuse or, as I have sometimes seen written in mid-range women's fashion publications, 'flirty', what would you make of that? Are you, perhaps, a regular Vogue reader?

John: Salient point, well made. Still. When can I see you in a dress that can neither be described by its owner nor understood by its aspiring remover in text?

Helen: When it is returned from an urgently needed dry-cleaning. The putrid frock will just have to be patient before playing its part in the acclaimed comedy Helen Becomes Big Dirty John's Internet Whore. Not now, clearly, as I imagine your plans at this late hour are set.

John: Not necessarily. I'm available. I have a cab fare. This may seem like the message of an eager teenager, which you already have, as you once complained, in over-supply. But I said I'm accommodating and I stick by that, irregardless of the consequences. (I can't believe my phone allowed that 'irregardless', but I'm kind of glad that it did.) I am accommodating, and I have been drinking.

Helen: John. Please keep in mind that I am A Lady. As such, my body is an object of exchange in the cruel economy of sex and I will have to apply lipstick, remove body hair and conceal my vaginal fangs and such. This would take a full hour.

John: An hour is fine, Chattel. Rehearsing one's gender performance and retracting one's teeth takes at least that long.

Helen: But I also have to feed my resentful, ageing and infirm sister a dead bird on a plate as I remember with regret my past as a glorious child star.

John: Well, I am required to manually type 'All Work and No Play Makes Jack a Dull Boy' in an endless range of literary formats as I plot to kill my family with an axe. We all have stuff to do, Helen.

To say that I took pleasure in John's messages is like saying that Kanye takes pleasure in himself. While I am conscious that their record may prompt you to ask 'Were you off your rocker?', I ask you to remember that I was.

But I was not so unsteady so as to actually admit this stranger to my home, however helpful this might have been to my need, and your hope, for a good story. An irresponsible act like that one would have provided us all with an excellent plot point. If I'd let him in, not even knowing his surname, you and I could agree that I had arrived at a nadir of recklessness and that now the only way was up. Especially if his dick hadn't worked and/or he'd tried to strangle me with this rope of non-functional dick.

It is true that I was reckless, but not so unthinking or devoted to story, as to return to a program of penis after so many years when its owner was avowedly drunk. The drunk dick was the thing that worried me. If I was going to change the stuff of my sex diet after so long, I wanted to be damn sure it would be a nourishing move. I longed, as I have said, to be back on solids.

The probability of liquid dick aside, I remained ambivalent about meeting John. This is not because I was still over-intellectualising the possibility and saying pseudo-psycho-analytic things to myself about writing and desire or whatever. This is not because I did not fully intend to get fully stuffed with cock—I remained, as I had for two days, unafraid of damage to either my person or my reputation.

It was chiefly because Text Message John had provided such excellent 'bating inspiration—or 'sinspiration', as I am sure I have seen a women's magazine call such stimulus—that I feared if he were to emerge from the gloom of his Dorothea Lange self-portrait, Physical John would provoke but a shadow of those excellent SMS-induced orgasms.

In any case, it was late. And this, being a Friday morning around 2 a.m., was the saddest time of the week for many people, but particularly for a newly dumped tool like me.

Sensibly, I stopped wanking and began to cry again. This time, I cried less forcefully than the bull-mastiff in critical condition. I cried more as a child who has just fallen does. First, I cried because of the pain, and then, less forcefully, with the memory of the pain. And then I cried just because I was crying and the tears had become their own *raison d'être*. I cried so much I dropped my phone and didn't even care to pick it up.

15

One week, 200 calories largely sourced from own snot, incalculable cry-wanks

In unsurprising news, the internet has a decent supply of freshly divorced middle-aged women in urgent want of cock. As such, I was not in the kind of high demand that would help me meet my goals on schedule. I had also not yet found the heart to amend my dating profile to something more appealing. So the Coldplay jokes remained.

I had been stubborn in achieving this state of dating mediocrity. But that did not mean I was happy to be overlooked as the irrelevance I certainly am.

I needed one hundred dates, and I wanted them *now*, though without immediate recourse to all the good advice about clean and plain speech I had previously received from Maddie and co. I was not yet ready to speak nicely—most especially after so much crying and children's theatre.

It had struck me that there was a community of people who may not only provide me with multiple dates, but who would actually appreciate dirty and elaborate dialogue. To wit, kinksters.

I had sworn off John. Well, this is entirely untrue. I had applied a brief John Moratorium. I had rebuffed his offer of drunk sex with the explanation that I would be at a 'work conference' for several days where the use of mobile devices was forbidden.

This was possibly a bit thick, as such a prohibition is unlikely applied these days in any professional environment outside the Situation Room. Possibly not even there. Those guys probably live-tweet the destruction of the Levant or text 'LOL Afghanistan' to their friends at Halliburton. Anyhow, I just wanted to stop nourishing my foul appetite for John and John's drunk penis *for a minute*, and I had decided that I wouldn't contact him at least until my shit-dress had returned from the cleaners.

I would provisionally replace John with as many members of the BDSM/Kink community as might consider me suitable for use/humiliation. And, no, I promise this had nothing to do with my reading of *Fifty Shades of Grey*. Which is not BDSM but virgin-fetish Barbara Cartland with fewer titled ladies and some unusual furniture. And which I had only ever read so I could make fun of it by text message with Celine. I would be sure to tell them I hated this book, just to prove that I wasn't some paperback tourist but a very earnest bottom. Hello, my name is Helen. I Am Not Anastasia Steele.

THE HELEN 100

I decided to attend a 'munch'.

A 'munch' does not refer to an afternoon of violent synchronised sex biting. Rather it is a meeting and dining opportunity for those who have joined, or seek to join, what is, regrettably, called 'The Lifestyle'. These events generally occur at a budget-eating establishment and do not involve what 'The Lifestylers' refer to as 'play'. Which is to say there is no guarantee of sex, but there is access to competitively priced tacos.

At a munch, one does not wear fetish finery nor speak at great volume about one's pressing urge to serve as a urinal. While some people may speak at low volume about the pleasure they take in their lavatory rank and others may be wearing an understated collar, it is agreed that in this 'vanilla' setting that the plain flavour of everyday behaviour will be generally observed.

The munch serves as a friendly get-together for the faithful as well as an open introduction for aspiring spankees and jizz buckets. And, of course, for those newbies who wish to administer the spanks and the jizz. But novices were not what I craved. I wanted to find an experienced Top who would comprehensively thrash me to within an inch of my safe word.

I had not quite decided yet if this safe word would be 'empowering' or 'feminism'. Or if longer phrases were permitted. 'It's Barbie's time to shine'?

The details for such munches are usually easy to locate on fetish dating sites, and, you know, I'd tell you on which password-protected site I found the time and place for mine if only I could remember my password first and hide a profile from you that, I recall, invited a swarthy Top to jizz in my face and call me his dirty little communist. No one outside the Kink community needs to see the rubbish I wrote. You'll just have to look up some munch details on your own.

I have some reservations about describing this event. Of course, I am obliged to do so as it represents seven per cent of my stupid goal of one hundred dates. But a queer lady does have *some* scruples when it comes to the possibly unfavourable, and probably unwanted, depiction of seven fellow perverts.

Which is to say, I don't enjoy making fun of people for their non-normative sexuality. I think that we queers already get enough bad press—unless, of course, we are Inspiring Homosexuals with rainbow babies who promote wholesome living on YouTube. Everybody loves those family-friendly guys.

I also do not wish to imply that these people are less discerning than others and so more inclined to bang a dickhead like myself. They certainly weren't desperate, unlike me. But I will say that my genuine sexual history of lesbianism played very well to the male Tops I had recently met online in the lead-up to the munch, and so I had become a more valuable commodity in this small marketplace than I had been in the broader economy of Dirty Divorcées. I was no longer in oversupply.

Of course, the Lesbian thing had proved popular on the more tedious adult dating sites as well, but none of those men had been eloquent enough to say, 'Beg me for my cock, queer.' A sentence, apparently, I had been longing to read.

THE HELEN 100

Before the event, I spoke for hours by online chat, and then by telephone, with a munch-coordinating Top we'll call Georges. Honestly, it was very hot: he was an interesting documentary filmmaker and he could spell 'anal' correctly. In fact, he caught onto my arousal by good punctuation and spelling early and proposed that if we met and we liked each other—or rather, 'If I consider a dyke like you worth hurting', which is a totally acceptable and hot thing to say in an emerging top-bottom hetero-flexible context—he would make me proofread his script treatments naked and not fuck my arse 'til I'd finished.

So I do not wish to make fun of these people. It would be both hypocritical and unkind.

Having said this, the whole thing (a) *was* mildly amusing, even to an opponent of normalised sexual codes and (b) it was not at all frightening. I figure that a description of this Bondage Beginners lunch date will serve less to malign its hosts than it will to encourage your possible future participation. I would certainly recommend this lunchtime introduction to Kink.

But I would offer a warning to my fellow Groucho Marxists: if you do not care to join a club that would admit you as a member, The Lifestyle is a place that will receive you fairly uncritically.

Membership doesn't sit well with me at all (that I frequently wish it did notwithstanding). But it just effing doesn't and the formal situations I have either left or been ejected from for non-compliance are too many to tally. A representative sample includes the Girl Guides, the Roman Catholic Church, school, the Communist Party, the Australian Broadcasting Corporation and two psychotherapists, but not Cheap Gerard who needed to hold on to his clients. One lawyer and an entire chain of garden superstores. And a marriage, obviously.

In short, I have often been thrown out of important things—or left as soon as I sensed the threat of ejection. This is no real brag of rebellion. It is simply an honest account of my regular failure to do as I should.

I do see the contradiction that arises when one both seeks and refuses discipline. The whole Problem with Authority thing needs to be overcome when one is, in fact, begging for authority. I did, quite earnestly, wish for some manageable pain and restraint: in this case of the sort that would perhaps provoke another's pleasure. But I didn't really want to be involved in anything referred to as 'The Lifestyle'.

Of course, more important than my personal issues with The Man were the matters of safety and consent. It's all well and good to want to be sexually or emotionally dominated—and I had wanted this unambiguous treatment for some time. Better the boot in the face, and all of that. But it's just dumb to accede to this domination without a set of guidelines, such as those The Lifestyle so amply provided. Rules all over the shop.

Nonetheless, it's also a bit difficult for a wad like me to say, 'I consent to not consenting', even though, obviously, this is the thing that every bottom must do. Otherwise the domination then ceases to be domination and becomes sexual assault—of which I am no fan.

These were the sorts of concerns I upheld before the munch, which was due to take place at a good, low-price south Indian restaurant in which I'd previously dined. If there was anything that would tempt me to eat again, it was the savoury pancake of southern India. So even if I didn't get admitted, or didn't want to be admitted to The Lifestyle, I would be sure to ingest some urgently needed carbohydrate. (I had eaten almost nothing since the ex left and I think that I was getting the ketosis breath that we can sometimes smell from the gobs of fad dieters.)

But no one was eating any carbs when I arrived, fifteen minutes late. The man who I recognised to be Georges, a man a tad diminished in height and athleticism since filling out his internet fetish profile, looked at me and said, 'Tsk.'

He was quite hot, quite small, and just starting to bald. For some reason, such natural tonsure in shortish men around fifty often makes me think, 'Ooh.' I'm not sure why. Perhaps because I think, 'Well, there's another shiny thing he can try to put inside my vagina.'

I said to Georges that I was sorry I was late and politely allowed the conversation to resume. Apparently, they had been talking about the matter of the service tip. Apparently, they did this too often.

'We do this too often,' said a youngish man with sandy lashes, who went on to explain *'again'* that he had developed a simple formula for the reliable calculation of a gratuity. Something about time spent dining plus or minus consensus about the quality of service divided by something or other.

'Oh, we can just *go* with it,' said a striking brunette person of indeterminate gender, who I later learned identified as a person of indeterminate gender. They were, according to their name tag, called 'Sam/Switch Hit', and I realised I had forgotten my own label and was called nothing at all.

Georges had previously explained that all the munchers must use name tags. Some like Sam/Switch used both their fetish name and their given name, while others, like the sandy boy, went only by 'Server', a reference both to his work in the IT industry, he would later explain, and to his peccadilloes.

'I'm sorry about my name tag,' I said.

Odette, a plump, pretty young lady with hot-magenta hair and gold skin, said, 'Georges's new girl is a silly little billy,' and grabbed my phone. She tapped 'MidLifeISIS' in the message app, magnified it with a nip of her Wüsthof nails and thrust it back my way. 'We were expecting you. Hold it up, noob,' she said with a stagey smile. Again, I said that I was sorry. Which I was.

I imagine that any aspiring kinkster, whether dominant or submissive, feels awkward in the first moments of a munch. I mean, you're sitting in an overly lit room made chiefly of Laminex with a group of people who all may reasonably suppose that your only passage to climax involves a diaper and a sprinkling of powder. And this is not, by any means, to disparage *any* hue of consensual human passion. It's all, as they say, good—even if you did buy it from a baby store. I have myself paused to find things just as strange as talcum arousing en route to fulfilment. Judge not lest ye be photographed wearing knitted booties on your dong, etc.

Nonetheless, the lights! Such stark illumination of all our dark urges made me uncomfortable. This was embarrassing in the short term, but probably a good sign for my sexual future. If the bright lights of this Indian restaurant had *failed* to make me uncomfortable, then it would mean my dark urges had perished.

Which is to say, for some of us, there can be no pleasure without dark guilt. I may have been asked to leave Mother Church, but she had never deserted me.

So, I was awfully, if necessarily, embarrassed.

I think this was okay, as blushing becomes a potential submissive. I was embarrassed, but also fairly sure that my embarrassment fit the role for which I had applied. I thought that it must be horrid to be a Top who suffers social anxiety, and that probably a lot of them do.

At any rate, MidLifeISIS was now red as the pile of chicken tikka—which the menu aficionado will note is not normally in the south Indian culinary repertoire. But it was there at the restaurant, in any case, as alien to its present environment as me.

Georges, who really was a decent-looking chap of the compact and well-proportioned sort that brings to mind the three-quarter copy function on an office Xerox machine, asked, 'Is that the name you want today?'

'That or Helen would do,' I said.

'Hello, Helen,' said a straight couple, neither of whom had heeded the vanilla dress code. This didn't mean that much in a city like this one, full of street theatre, but, still, I found their choice of the blacksmith's aprons unsettling. He was called 'Anvil' and she was called 'Hammer', and neither of these tools had, in my view, done much to honour discretion. Not that discretion was something that I gave much thought to at the time, but the rules of the munch *had* been written fairly clearly and that this pair had seen fit to come in bearing a placard that basically said 'We're Going to Fuck You In a Blast Furnace' was a clear violation.

Still, I guess I hadn't worn a name tag. I held up my phone screen in an effort to stick to the rules.

There was another chap present. He was about forty, he wore a lot of denim all at once and his name tag said 'Stumpy'. I initially supposed that this name signified his fondness for erotic humiliation. There are those chaps, I had read, who enjoy having their penis size derided. Again, good luck to these men from whom I can claim no distance. I was myself aroused by the thought of editing someone's screenplay while earning no money and wearing no pants. And also, apparently, by being broken up with, by residual Catholic shame and by a range of other items and practices that even I am not so foolish as to disclose.

Stumpy, as it turned out, was not one of those who craved a verbal beating. He was, in fact, an aspiring Master and Stumpy was not really his fetish name but an everyday sobriquet acquired when he had lost half his leg in a boating incident; an absence I hadn't immediately noticed. And, no, of course I didn't ask. What sort of nuff goes about asking a one-legged man, 'Where did you leave your limb?' He had told me about it when he asked if I wouldn't mind popping up and ordering him a dosa.

'Rather not do it myself if I can help it,' he said and he patted his stump. 'Boat. That's why I'm Stumpy. No left leg, love. I left him in the sea.'

'I hear you have a third leg, anyhow,' said Odette. Everyone cackled. Although Georges and Sam seemed to do so only out of duty. Stumpy just went deadpan, like the Buddha.

There was, as far as I knew, no written agenda for the meeting. Still, it seemed to proceed along a course familiar to its participants, who were all regulars except for me. They spoke of past Lifestyle events. They spoke of upcoming Lifestyle events. They complained a little about the quality of music at some Lifestyle events and Sam said, 'I am sick to the back fangs of that hideous, nineties industrial drone. I mean, who wants to hear mechanical bashing and feel like they're trapped inside a foundry? No offence, Hammer.'

'None taken. I couldn't agree more about Skinny Puppy. I would say it's the sound a fax machine makes before it dies.'

Some of them were a little lewd and free with double entendre, but not much of it was racier than a *Carry On* film. Not even from Anvil or Hammer. This wasn't X-rated. A few of them talked about a recent Shibari workshop and Georges offered the opinion that the *alleged* rope artist was not to be trusted with the quality of his knots, which had not, he had it on good authority, even been studied in Japan.

I tried to focus on the idea of being tied up by handsome little Georges, even in knots of dubious nationality. I tried to catch his eye. But I wasn't really meshing with this sex lunch for a couple of reasons.

First, Anvil had dropped some coconut sambal on his collar, and I found this distracting. It looked like jizz. Second, I felt like I had been in a similar situation before and I couldn't quite place it.

When Hammer hissed—affectionately, it should be said—at Anvil, 'You're a dirty little man-baby who can't be trusted with his dinner,' I remembered. This felt a bit like a pyramid sale for kitchen appliances.

A few years before, I had been required by work to take notes at one of those Tupperware-like events. You know, the sort of thing where ladies' homes are used as a party-plan store. The gathering is intended as both a social event and a point of sale, but it fails to be completely one or the other. It may succeed at the time as a sale in terms of hard cash, but no one ever really feels that they weren't obliged to buy, and this sensation of pressure always diminishes the social experience, which in turn diminishes the esteem in which the purchased product is held, and future sales do not follow. As such, the blender I had been commissioned to falsely praise in print is no longer sold.

(This is clearly not the case for Tupperware, which is a fucking awesome product. Tupperware continues to have great use-value and no volume of terrible parties will ever change this. To be clear, I have no financial interest in the Tupperware corporation and I have myself insufficient funds to afford even more than two pieces of Tupperware. Nonetheless, I admire Tupperware, which is as durable and as timeless in design as are the knotted ropes of the very best Japanese perverts.)

This party plan comparison struck me not because I felt that The Lifestylers were evangelising or even soft-selling their noble crafts. Not like that lady with her hand-held blender. 'Look. You can make breadcrumbs,' she had said, as though anyone ate carbs anymore outside southern India. The munch wasn't *that* disconnected from the social. But I did get a sense there of the social connection that is slowly frayed by business, or perhaps of the force of the trade economy, which leaves its impression even on our private economies of love and friendship.

But there *had* to be a sort of businesslike element here, too. I soon became aware, and remain respectful, of the responsible approach the Kink community takes to its activity. It's sensible to meet your fellows in a vanilla environment and heavens knows what might happen if kinksters only met while wearing gimp suits and holding bedpans. Kink relationships, especially those that involve the receipt of pain, need to have their guidelines set well away from the rack. You don't just jump in arse-first and hope to get exactly the kind of beating you can stand.

Still, I couldn't help but be a little disappointed by the Tupperware approach. The Lifestyle seemed to be a place where the love we might find for each other was discussed, demonstrated and burped in advance. Call me a romantic, but I craved spontaneity in a thrashing.

The meeting drew to a close. I stayed close to compact, muscular Georges. He had given excellent internet chat and would, it seemed to me, also give an excellent dose of what-for should he deem me and my arse worth the time. But in those few minutes after the meeting that I begged to spend with him, I saw that I was not up to fetish snuff.

I mean, *perhaps* he found me tolerably attractive. I was, after all, wearing a dress entirely free of cat waste. I also have the sort of skin that any connoisseur of violence would know bruises easily, and I imagine this would be a plus. But even if he had deemed me physically desirable, I was perhaps not his type of girl. Not in my reckless, unbusinesslike state.

We walked towards the railway station and then he beckoned me to the old steps that led down to the Yarra. As we descended, he placed his hand, lightly but assertively enough for me to know I was still in with an eighth of a chance, on the small of my back, and growled, in not an unappealing way, 'What the fuck do you want?'

'Um. To be dominated?' I said.

He rolled his eyes, and his body, which a moment before had been straining towards me and the river, fell halfway back into repose. He said, 'FFS. Be more specific,' and then grabbed and pulled my ponytail quite hard and spun me around so that my back was now against the old wall that runs by the riverbank.

(This, I ought to report, was an act of address to which I had already consented with Georges by internet message. The BDSM people were terribly organised about their brutality.)

Be more specific. Well, I was more specific. As I felt him pull on my hair and resume his interest, by which I mean cock, I was able to say some really specific shit.

It's not so much that I will not offer an account of this filth, I am just unable to recall it. It was a great stream of Kerouac Kink written on a single sheet of longing—the sort of tosh that seems ridiculous and begs to be forgotten everywhere but in its very particular moment. All I can really remember is that it involved a lot of 'arse', 'fuck' and 'hurt me, Georges', and possibly an offer from me to clean his kitchen in my scanties.

For a good thirty seconds, this seemed to go down pretty well. He pulled my hair with one hand and grabbed my wrist with another and I felt quite fixed against the old retaining wall. As he Vader-breathed into my ear, he positioned himself against me with mocking expertise—which is to say, he was the sort of chap sufficiently fascinated by sex and its preamble that he seemed to have learned just where and how a fully dressed boner should prod a lady so that she would begin to feel quite faint. I can tend to be a fairly coarse person, but I was momentarily well mannered as I said, 'Please, Georges. *Please.*'

And then, I do remember, that I said that I wanted him to blow in my arse after he had finished whacking it with one of his devices. And he said, 'Yeah, I'll put on a condom and blow in your arse,' and I said, 'No condoms. I want you to come inside me,' and, well, that was it. Au revoir, Monsieur Bataille and friends. Twelve down. Eighty-eight dates to go.

'Bareback? Are you mad?' he said.

Well yes, I was, as we have amply established. Still, I thought I was being super hot and that my genuine invitation to transgress the recommended health practice for casual hook-ups was extra super hot. But the transgression specialist knows that any compromise to safety is also a compromise to future transgression and, again, I was terribly impressed by Kink's commitment to Best Practice. But, you know, disappointed that a fairly bright and hot chap wasn't going to sodomise me with what seemed to be an organ of notable girth.

I apologised and tried not to cry. Georges said that he too was sorry and asked me if something stressful had recently unfolded in my life. And then, of course, I did cry and the poor chap ended up having to sit me down, listen to the account of my break-up and buy me a Starbucks. And, I really don't think a Smoked Butterscotch Latte was what he'd cycled into the city that day to find.

Nonetheless, this was a decent man who now gave me some decent advice, in lieu of unsafe sex.

He said that BDSM was not the place where you sought a cure to your past woes. It was, or it should be, more a place where you played them out at an advanced level, having already done some elementary work. He told me how his father had been a cruel man. He told me that codifying his own dominance in a very conscious way with women made him a much better feminist. If he played out the masculine brutality in his memory, he found he was able to release the real forms of it from his everyday behaviour. But, he said, it was important that he knew that this was what he was doing *well* before he actually started doing it.

'I swear, without BDSM, I could have become a Men's Rights dick,' he told me, and I certainly saw the logic here. Get rid of the power by continually laying it bare.

BDSM practice is not an aberration. BDSM is, in my view, a good attempt at honesty. Responsibly done, it is conscious engagement with one's past and shouldn't be a chaotic, condom-free game of pin-the-tail-on-the-repressed-donkey. You open your eyes to the repression first, *then* you sit in a well-lit Indian restaurant after having first stared the ass in the face. Apparently, I hadn't identified my herd of problems.

Georges gave me the good advice to sort out my shit before I returned to this community, one I now esteemed as an exemplary self-regulator. Goodness, if the construction industry could only apply itself even half as well as the kinksters do in upholding safety guidelines there'd never be another on-site injury again.

I tried to kiss him once more in the Starbucks. I was crying and, as he pointed out, I had a snout full of caramel froth, which probably looked like santorum. He told me I wasn't ready to be kissed, much less beaten.

'Sort out your shit, Helen.'

I thanked Georges for the company, the advice and the Grande, and even managed not to get all huffy and explain that I *was* trying to sort out my shit, thanks, and that I had a Helen One Hundred spreadsheet to prove it. Instead, I bowed my head to Master and made my way to the train that would return me to my miserable half-home.

I turned my phone off so I could think through several stations. I thought about how things might have been better between the ex and me if we'd made time to communicate outside diplomatic channels. If we'd owned up to our different kinds of power instead of pretending that love could ever be democratic. If we'd either (a) attended a Japanese rope bondage workshop or (b) admitted that one of us was always in control of the money and the other was always in control of the love. If only we knew who was wearing which boots. If only we had been brutal and honest.

And then I got bored, as others rightly did, with my tortured thinking and I just turned the damn phone on again so I could let the shit of life sort me out for a spell, rather than the more demanding reverse.

John: Trust the conference is thrilling.

Helen: Goodness, but there is nothing I love more than an inspirational speech with PowerPoint. Briefly. Do you mind if I learn your last name? Please feel at your ease in replying 'no'.

John: Not at all. I urge you to Google-stalk me and learn just how very dull I am. It's John Blank.

Helen: Oh, I don't care at all to check your credentials. I'm just picking out names for our baby. I think it should be Sharon, even if male. Sharon Razer-Blank.

John: Somehow Razer-Blank brings to mind press gangs on the Cornish coast of the 1800s.

Helen: Look, I'm currently in professional company and you know you get me hot when you make historical reference to organised enslavement.

John: As we know, it's the origin story of every hot Australian male. How's the food at the conference?

Helen: I'm afraid I've signed a morning tea non-disclosure agreement and am obliged to remain silent on the matter of pinwheel sandwiches. Oh, goodness. I've already said too much. We'll continue making our plans for little Sharon's education at a Steiner school as soon as I am done with the secret snacks.

John: Are they all gluten free? If so, be careful not to breastfeed. Sharon has an allergy to wheat. Poor little thing. I look forward to our discussion of her grain alternatives and alternative education. Next week, perhaps?

I selected a winking emoji and then erased it. I was far too old for this sort of code and I could never be certain which of the colourful glyphs did not represent a penis. I supposed that all of them could stand in for the culture's threshold symbol, depending on the conversation. Best not to send anything. Following my obscenities to Georges, I had decided to make the effort to clean my communication of 'cock'. I mean, if you've just offended a dungeon master with your language, it's probably time for some sort of Swiss finishing school.

I returned to find Eleven in a tabby ball on top of the dry-cleaned khaki frock. 'I am unmoving,' he said, and multiplied his mass by gravity when I tried to lever him off. I lay down beside this dependable force and began an account of my afternoon. He said we was unmoved.

16

Two weeks, one overworked android

Kay, with whom I had spoken by telephone, had attempted to contact me several times to talk about recovery. She eventually texted in ANGRY MAJUSCULE.

> **Kay:** FUCKING RAZER. YOU COCK. MY SPIRIT ANCESTOR SAYS I NEED TO TALK TO YOU ABOUT YOUR PROBLEMS. DON'T FUCK WITH MY SPIRIT ANCESTOR.

Kay was an acquaintance with a bag of new-agey tricks and a great willingness to perform these whenever she felt there was a chance. When I had spoken with her a few days back, she had insisted she would come to my house to 'smudge' it of bad feeling.

Smudging is a practice derived from America's First Nation peoples and involves setting fire to a stick of dried sage, which doesn't smell like the stuff you put on a beef roast at all. The sage, said Kay, would be lethal to bad divorce energy. It would also prove fatal to what little survived of my appetite.

Kay had said that she was on her way and she'd pick me up from the train station—I'd returned from date number thirteen, which was with a guitarist I had known a bit for decades. I shan't go into detail as this poor, dear lass, who I had always liked and even rather fancied, was in a worse state than me. Let it be said, however, that meth is not good for any person, save for psychotic kingpin, Tuco Salamanca.

I was surprised Kay drove a Jeep Grand Cherokee. I really thought she'd be the hybrid type. I must have looked lost as I abseiled into the enormous vehicle because she said, 'Hideous, isn't it? Came free with the last reality gig I did on TV.'

As promiscuous in her spiritual affiliations as I was hoping to be with my vagina, Kay believed in many things other than sage, including the power of Wiccan ritual, intricate conspiracies by major seed companies and the effectiveness of the Twelve Step program.

'After we smudge, we're going to have a really good talk about the program.'

This sentence, which stands as the best harbinger of hippy tedium I've ever heard, was the one Kay uttered as she sped into my street.

THE HELEN 100

This was not the first time she'd recommended the twelve steps. They were important to her, and she firmly held that they could be important to everybody else.

At a past interval, Kay had developed a heavy drinking habit and this gradually became an unbearable weight. It was when she, a person of some media prominence, appeared in a newspaper blind item that described her pissing during the dinner rush in the nitrogen bath of a then-popular chef while singing the hits of Rodgers and Hart (this was more-or-less true, although it was a lunch service, she pissed on a live southern rock lobster and was belting hits from *Phantom*) she determined to get 'clean'.

This, in my view, was a bit of a shame because what is lunch at high-end city restaurants if it does not include loud urinating celebrity patrons who are half woman, half pinot grigio and all 'The Music of the Night'? I still found the story delightful and I was sad that anyone would consider it a case of 'hitting bottom'.

Still, I imagine it's troubling to be unable to recall one's fifty-dollar entrée that would later be lost to a toilet, so it is no real tragedy that Kay tried several different methods to clean her blood. She eventually found Alcoholics Anonymous to provide the best transfusion.

Not to get too judgey (because, after all, who was I if not some wretched tart who couldn't keep her relationship alive, her mouth civil or her vagina/anus filled), but Kay had seemed to form an addiction to the address of addictive patterns.

She had spoken to me in the past about AA et al. with troubling reverence. The steps contained the cure and the explanation for *everything*. Or everything that couldn't be set to rights with herbs and clairvoyance.

Of course, twelve-stepping is a much healthier and cheaper thing to binge on than booze and surely all of us are creatures that consistently exchange our large anxieties for smaller models. We all try to downsize our worry. We try to trade big problems for slighter ones. This manageable, structured fear is at work when, say, we ignore a crushing deadline and decide to clean out our sock drawer instead.

This is perhaps what my former partner had done when selecting my younger, less difficult replacement from a Facebook page. This is what we do when our relationships have turned to shit and we invite Kay into our homes to trade our break-up stink for a fog of sage.

She produced some matches, a bag of salt and a mother-of-pearl shell from a bag that, she told me, was made by Nepalese women.

'Set your intention,' she said, and fished out an oblong wad of dried plant.

'Um,' I said.

'Shit, Helen. What do you want me to smudge?'

Kay had asked this as though I'd made a formal smudging request, which I had not. I didn't know how to guide the matter and as someone who had lately become a fairly literal and childish listener, was quite confused when she asked again, 'What do you want cleared by a smudging from this house?'

I very much doubted that smudging was an accurately translated Native American term. I also doubted that 'smudged' or 'cleared' could be words used in close association.

Surely smudging and clearing are, if not actual opposites then at least vastly different verbs. 'To smudge' is not to clear but to obfuscate by smearing around, and who wants that? Even if we do accept this mistranslation and believe that smudging can provide clarity, what's the point of clarity?

All the 'clarity' of the past weeks had been unbearable. I just kept seeing unvarnished truths—I was a failed whore, I was a greenhorn pervert, I was a mean partner—and nearly every time I saw these things, I cried. I'd had more than enough clarity. I'd produced many smudges, not all of which could be removed by the drycleaner.

'Tell me what you want.'

At some point I hoped people would stop asking me that, and start telling me what I wanted. I had no clue.

I refrained from telling Kay that the sage stick looked like Satan's pubic hair. I determined to receive Kay's pungent gift with hope. Why shouldn't I? I reminded myself of all the money I had spent that first night on tele-shamanism from Reykjavik and reasoned that at least this afternoon of stinky bullshit was free of charge. So I told her what I probably wanted: my guilt gone from the kitchen, the worst memories of my partnership out of the bedroom, and the smell of Sandra's twat exiled from the shed.

Kay spread salt in several doorways, lit the devil's merkin with the matches and set it in one shiny half of the former home of a deceased gastropod. 'Mother Ocean, source of all life,' she said. Which weren't words that troubled me too much because they, in an evolutionary sense, could sort of be said to be true.

'I call all the angels,' Kay said as she moved in a clockwise—sorry, *sunwise*—direction. 'I call the ancestors and the animal spirits and the Lord Jesus Christ.'

As she cast her circle and assembled a group of divine beings a little too assorted to be able to settle their differences in my dirty house, I just gave in. A bunch of twigs had exactly as much power to clear/smudge 'bad energy' as one decided that they should, and I made a real effort to push the scientific Marx out of my mind (he would not approve of this mystic fetishism at all).

But Marx was not the authority on everything. Kay was the authority on everything.

By the time she was forty, Kay had attended most iterations of the Twelve Step program. Among those she had embraced were Love and Sex Addicts Anonymous, Overeaters Anonymous, Rageaholics Anonymous, Narcotics Anonymous, Gamblers Anonymous and Al-Anon, the support group for friends and family of alcoholics. It was this group Kay would advise me to attend.

Actually, when I first told Kay about the Helen One Hundred—and, as we know, I couldn't stop talking about everything to anyone who gave me half a shell back then—she said I should probably go to Love and Sex Addicts Anonymous as well.

'You have a real problem with wanting to be loved,' said Kay.

I didn't think it was a problem then. I still don't.

I told her, as she waved the herb sausage about the place, that one set of twelve steps would be sufficient. 'If I have to be something, I'll be the Former Partner of an Alcoholic,' I said.

I shouldn't have said this. I shouldn't have told Kay that my ex was an alcoholic *again*. I shouldn't have even thought of my ex as an alcoholic. It was unfair. It was unkind. If I had suffered the pain and lived with knowledge of the course of a shitty, incurable disease, I might turn to drink, too. Heck, I might even start cheating, making assemblages and seeking the right to 'grow'.

I shouldn't have said she was an alcoholic. But you just say stuff when you're newly dumped. You say everything. You say, 'Fuck my arse without a condom,' 'I am frightened of vaginas,' or 'Take your wart of a job and send it to the arse doctor, Brynlee.'

Public Service Announcement: If you have been newly dumped, please watch out for this rotten tendency to Tell the Truth. Please. If you don't, you might very well find yourself saying things like, 'Sometimes I wake in a cold sweat screaming for death'—a sentence I had added to the 'hobbies' section of my internet dating profile that morning.

(This truth, incidentally, did not produce a positive result. Some internet chap with a thing for pseudo-necrophilia saw it and messaged, 'Great! We can pretend that you're dead!' He then offered to pop over, fill my bathtub with ice into which I would slide, and ten minutes later be lifted from fake dead so he could fake rape my fake corpse. Again, not to judge. But (a) this interaction didn't even take place on the fetish site where it properly belonged and (b) NO.

People don't need to know everything about you, and you can't expect them to react favourably when you tell them your unfortunate shit. (Although I will say that the unwelcome offer of fake rape of your fake corpse is hardly ever going to be your fault.)

I know I said everything and I am now writing almost everything, but I am committing this dreadful account to print for your own damn good. Do as I say, and not as I did. I am your cautionary woman. You who are newly dumped need to learn to zip it, just like I didn't. Because truth sets you free only as much as booze will. Which is to say, it feels great at the time, but you are guaranteed regret and pain after the falsely liberating indulgence.

Truth. What a crock.

THE HELEN 100

Goodness how I talked in those post-separation weeks, and I say this as one who is a championship-league talker. I said everything to everyone even more often than I normally do. I told Kay about how I had jacked the ex's Facebook account and learned of her several affairs, how I couldn't stand the ex's mispronunciation of several words but most especially 'arbiter', which she said as though it rhymed with 'car biter'. I also told Kay how the ex and I had once taken a three-way vacation in New York with a libertarian Yale alumnus in a misguided effort towards DIY couples' therapy.

So she probably wasn't all wrong to recommend the Love and Sex Addicts Anonymous group.

Look. I shouldn't have told Kay about this and I certainly shouldn't be telling you, but I've started now and, as it perhaps seems unlikely to you that I will ever get nailed again, let me tell you about one time that I did.

17

Before she left, one diagnosis
This whole three-way thing started five years ago, after the ex's first CT scan.

On that day, which I am unlikely to forget, the person who was then my partner had said, 'I really don't like the way the radiographer looked at me.' Two hours later, the GP had said, 'I really don't like the look of this lesion on your right frontal lobe.' Then the neurologist in the emergency ward said, 'I really don't like the idea of you going home tonight.' She was admitted as a patient.

We asked if it was really necessary. He said 'yes' and then the words 'possible fatal seizure', and I tried to pack her a useful case of things for hospital.

'Why did you bring me napkin rings?' she said from the bed when I'd returned.

After she'd been in the hospital for a day, she needed a drink. I sprang her from the neurosurgery ward and took her to the pub for a beer. After just one, she failed her reflex exam. We had honestly thought that a drink would improve things.

'Something is wrong, baby,' she said.

The doctors agreed. Something *was* wrong and the next week passed in serology and fear. There was a lumbar puncture, which despite the fact it hurt her like the dickens, is now a procedure I can never think of without affection.

The neurologist, who was a big, young, goofy Czech chap, showed us the spinal tap needle and said, with a doofus grin, 'Now, where do I put this again?' She laughed. He asked her if she liked *The Simpsons*. When she said that she did, he yelled, 'Hi everybody! I'm Doctor Nick!', who is a *Simpsons* extra well known for provoking malpractice suits with his whacky medical mistakes. Our Czech then swung the comically enormous thing around, again announcing that he was Doctor Nick, and while she, the nurse who was pinning her down and I were all laughing hard, he stuck it in her back and drained her cerebral fluid. Like all good jokes, this one came at a risk.

Other than that, it was a terrible week. It was the week I learned to pronounce terms like 'metastasis', which sounds a bit like 'Minneapolis', and 'cysticercosis', which sounds almost exactly like 'sister psychosis', a mondegreen that now serves as the name for my imaginary feminist dubstep project. (My first fictitious release is called Schizoaffective Rimjob, in whose promotional image I appear naked but for a bite mask for the criminally insane.)

It was a terrible week.

It was the week that ended when they uttered one last term. She heard it. She didn't cry. I jogged off to the family room where I crouched behind a broken gurney and howled.

On the way home in the car, she said, 'This is what I have to deal with now.'

If you had seen her, you would have applauded. I loved her so much.

As for my performance: the notices were pretty bad. I went back to work two days later and told a famous international actor I was interviewing to go and fuck himself. They talked about this 'outrage' in the newspaper and on TV, even though this was an actor who had been told, quite justifiably, to fuck himself a number of times. I guess it was a slow news week. I lost my job. The ex had lost so much more than that, but kept on acting beautifully.

The next few years were interchangeably blank or false and always a bit airless. She travelled alone to Spain, Mauritius, Ireland, Uzbekistan, Finland, or wherever funds, now derived from a series of soul-fucking jobs I performed while grumbling, would allow her to travel.

She started drinking a lot and I began to suspect that she wasn't feeling serene or evolved at all. Through these years, she often said that she refused to be a victim, a patient, the effect of medical institutions. She had often said that she was writing her way out of this one and had me convinced of her literary transcendence. 'I refuse to be an inspiration,' she had said. It was inspiring. I was envious of the book her brave pain promised to produce.

On at least one of these flights far away from our still marriage, she cheated on me. She didn't want to sleep with me, so she slept with other people. She didn't enjoy her real life with me, so she had a false life with happier people. It was expensive and it was humiliating.

I can't blame her. But I blame her.

When she was ready to explain why a young Scandinavian had written on her Facebook page 'I have you for pussy party anytiem!!', she said that she *had* cheated on me, but that she'd prefer to cheat on me next time while I was actually in the room. We would do this abroad, she said. We would put the sex back into this marriage. And perhaps some of the marriage back, too.

Her appetites were stimulated by travel and its prospect. At that sexless point in my life, my appetites were stimulated by anything at all. So, if I was going to get laid—and, I really do like sex quite a lot—it had to be in another nation with an extra person.

'But a *stranger*, Helen?' said Kay.

I reminded Kay that it was a far better plan to have a three-way with a stranger than, say, one of the idiots from my office. I did not remind Kay that back in the nineties, she was herself widely celebrated for fucking first and failing to ask questions later. This, in any case, would have just given her licence to talk about her grand program of reform and how Love and Sex Addicts Anonymous had cured her of the youthful need for nooky. So I just told Kay about the time I had a three-way with a 'stranger'.

Public Service Announcement: If you *are* considering a three-way with your partner, I am going to insist that you select a participant unknown to both of you, and preferably one with whom the likelihood of close future contact is nil. Further, there are those who should consider not doing this at all. If your intention is to spice a marriage that has lost its flavour for sad and complex reasons, then the solution is perhaps *not* to go and mutually fuck someone else. Especially not in an expensive hotel thousands of kilometres away from your home.

Look. Do whatever you want. Just try to not be the dick that I am.

I told Kay that we had found him on the internet without much trouble at all. We were two relatively fuckable female tourists who had promised to return to our nation after the fucking was complete. Quite fathomably, we were a convenience in high demand. Such high demand, in fact, that we were able to make a shortlist consisting entirely of former Ivy Leaguers, all of whom had graduated with Latin honours. We actually settled on a *summa cum laude,* just for the elitist hell.

'No! Not how did you find him. How did you *find* him?'

Miss Abstinence wanted to know about the sex.

Kay had now taken a prurient rather than a moral interest in my account. This was fine with me. Perhaps she'd get a bit hot under her Spanx and we could have a tussle, as we had sometimes done in the nineties. She could go to a meeting to recover.

Even if we didn't have a snog, I decided that this afternoon was now intimate enough to count as a date. Fourteen down. Eighty-six to go.

'Look, I've cleared your bad energy. The least you can do is give me something fucked-up to report to my sponsor,' said Kay.

I briefly wondered if 'report to my sponsor' could serve me in future as a comic euphemism for masturbation. Then I said that the sex was 'good and bad', and next I just asked her, 'Why the fuck are *you* asking *me*, anyhow?'

I mean, if anyone knew what a three-way was like, it was Kay, who had graduated from slut school *Come Loudly*. Boom tish.

'You've had more three-ways than my Aunty Joan has had communion wafers,' I told her.

This was true. If I didn't count the seven kinksters I'd just met, no person of my immediate acquaintance had partaken of the bodies of so many.

Kay said, 'I can't remember any of it. If only I could remember a bit of all the fucked-up sex I had, I might still be able to have fucked-up sex. As it is, I'm in meetings for being a drunk sex addict seven days a week. So, the least you can do is tell me about your fucked-up sex.'

I first told Kay that this three-way was okay, but that I couldn't recommend it as especially therapeutic. I then told her, in my tedious way, that this was not because I believed that consensual adventurous sex is intrinsically bad. All pleasure that is safe and consensual is good pleasure . . .

'Shut up with your extreme sexual tolerance, you bitch, and tell me about his cock.'

'Look, Kay. I will try to remember some juicy stuff, but there's one terrible image that really gets in the way of the good ones. The fact is, my ex looked like she was waiting for a bus. She was getting this head-job from a very handsome, and quite twitchy, young Yale graduate, but she looked exactly like she was waiting for a bus.'

That's just how she had looked. Like she was waiting for something to take her away. Honestly, I think this dude was probably much better at cunnilingus than me. He seemed to be a methodical type of thinker, possibly even one with a dash of neurodevelopmental disorder. *Hot*. In any case, I'm positive he would have done a lot of reading to prepare for this 'encounter', as dirty sex derived from the personal ads is known in the United States.

They do love to name things in the register of Personal Growth, those Americans. They also love to prepare for an event. If you want something formalised and studied and described in the language of empowerment, call an American.

As far as I could tell, this Yale guy was carpet munching with all the skill and willingness of someone who had just completed a degree. I mean, he clearly had laboratory-tested techniques going on. There was absolutely no reason, in my view, for her to look as bored as she did.

This is the problem with the three-way. It can reveal your partner at unflattering angles.

After the 'encounter', I asked the ex about this face of hers, rationally fearful that she endured my almost certainly inferior head jobs with exactly that look, if not one of even greater unconcern. She told me that she couldn't help it, and, incidentally, that my sex face was hardly any better. Apparently, when he was doing me from behind and I was going down on her—a classic FFM three-way configuration—the top half of my face looked like that of a very simple child smiling for a school photograph.

So, if we'd never had this 'encounter', we could have gone on believing that each of our sex expressions were just like those of the ecstatic ladies in porn. Instead we spent a lot of money to find that during sex one of us looked like a complaisant fifth-grade idiot and the other looked like a jaded teenager.

'Get to the fucked-up sex,' said Kay, who seemed to keep veering between judgement, boredom and arousal.

I wished that I could.

'Okay,' I said. 'So he spun me 'round and fucked me hard from behind without so much as a BY YOUR LEAVE, MA'AM.' She sat beside us and put a hand over my mouth so that I could not scream, as I am wont to do. She then sat on a chair across the room and watched him make me come. She told him to fuck my arse, which he wouldn't, but it was arousing in any case to hear this request. She told me to go down on him and when I did, she returned and guided my head up and down on him with her hands to the point that I thought that I might choke.

This was the nearest approach we had ever made to replicating our relationship in sex, but the proto-BDSM kick was not sufficient to save us.

'Is that enough? I can't remember much else.' Just as I was unable to find sex in my present life, I was having difficulty locating it in my past. 'I mean, I know it was mostly quite good and that he definitely spoodged on my chest.'

I certainly knew that I enjoyed some of the 'encounter'. But something corroded my memory a bit. I also had come to know that it took place in a hotel that, two years later, would become a fairly infamous crime scene where a worker alleged she had been sexually assaulted by a guest, who happened to be a director of the International Monetary Fund.

I was sad at the thought of what may have happened to this worker, employed to clean up after vacation sluts like me, but I was also pretty shitty with the IMF whose lending policies were, in my view, just as brutal as the alleged assault.

This revulsion I had for the finance sector's habit of fucking the workers of the world induced a sort of pleasure-amnesia. My memories of the 'encounter' became quickly hazy.

'I can't remember much else,' I added, 'except that all this occurred not so long after the 2008 crash.'

'Jesus, Helen. Do you have to bring money into everything? Even sex?'

I know the question Kay had asked was a fair one. But I had long been of the view that money has the habit of bringing itself into everything, with no kind of help from me, and especially into a sex holiday that had cost thousands of dollars. And one, moreover, that took place in the world's financial centre *and* had itself produced a conversation about money. Specifically, the need for gold to resume its place as the standard unit of US account.

I didn't ask this Yale alumnus to reveal himself as a Gold Standard libertarian. But he did.

Between three-ways, he said that he believed in gold, and that Nixon had ruined this country. Naturally, an argument between him and me about currency and the responsibility of the state followed. She told me to 'Shush' and 'Leave the money out of it for once, Helen.'

The Skull and Bones man soon forgot that we'd been arguing about the convertible dollar, because my girlfriend was now administering what looked like a virtuosic hand job. Which, I supposed, was something a girl learns at a good private school.

'Ladies, this is what you do when a Marxist harpy has argued politics with your successful husband.' Pump. Pump.

But I kept on talking and this killed his third boner. As we have now established, I am the sort of person who ruins sexual adventure with my economic views.

'This money thing is a compulsion and I am very embarrassed about it,' I said to Kay.

'Yes. But you should also be embarrassed about having sex with a stranger.'

'Oh, shut up. I'm not embarrassed in front of you.'

I am sufficiently socialised to know that the thing I should be most embarrassed about disclosing here—to *you* and not to Kay, who was a famous slut and therefore, despite her moral presentations, actually unshockable—is not my uncontrollably boring views on money but that my female partner and me not only had sex with but *planned and bought aeroplane tickets* in order to have sex with an age-inappropriate student of bullshit in a hotel that was so expensive it would later host a director of the IMF.

Of course I am embarrassed when I think about this terrible couples' therapy. Mostly because this freedom fanboy turned out to be engaged to a young woman who, as I discovered later by internet, had won an award for selfless dedication to the New York public school system.

This promising person clearly had no clue about her partner's activities, which were misrepresented to her by text message after one round of sex had ended and another one had begun to seem very likely.

He recited semi-consciously as he wrote, 'Stuck at Habitat for Humanity', a charitable organisation to which, he had told us previously by internet message, he often volunteered his service as a construction worker.

In the midtown suite, I began to feel very bad for the people whose low-cost homes would be built by Ivy League hands unaccustomed to labour but that were now familiar with my arsehole. I also felt bad for Habitat for Humanity, whose reputation had been exploited in the service of infidelity. But I felt the worst for his girlfriend; her most intimate bond violated through the ridiculous attempt to intensify my own.

So there was one positive reading of my three-way, which I urged Kay to consider, hoping it might stop her from insisting I go to one of those damn Sex Addicts meetings: As soon as I saw him texting his girlfriend, I did my best to stop further sex.

I wasn't able to completely stop it. I mean, we'd spent *so much* money to get there.

I couldn't stop this sex, therefore diminishing its quality was the only moral course, but for the sake of low-cost housing providers and of the partners of the people engaged to their duplicitous volunteers I made sure that we all had an ordinary time.

I am sure the libertarian never looks back to part three, possibly part four, of our 'encounter' fondly. I lay there like a starfish in the hope he would be so struck by my mediocrity that he would never cheat again. I also farted.

'Are you ashamed?' asked Kay.

I couldn't say that I was ashamed either of the bad sex or the farting. Anyhow, at that point, my shame would have made about as much sense as a violent sectarian militia leader apologising for mispronouncing the word *Kalashnikov* on YouTube. I'd incriminated myself with filth and with infidelity. What was a fart, now?

I told her that I was not ashamed of the 'encounter'. But that I was ashamed of my lack of due diligence, which should have turned up the fact of the libertarian's fiancée (and the fact that he was a libertarian).

Sure, it's true that he had said in his dating profile that he was single but, then again, we had described ourselves as a 'happy couple'. I should have known better. I should have known that people lie when they shouldn't, and forget to lie when they should.

Kay finally agreed that I was clearly more of a sex saboteur than a sex addict. Especially when I told her about Anton and Georges. But since she was such a big fan of the program, she insisted that she drive me to an Al-Anon meeting.

After failing to give her anything much she could 'report to her sponsor', I figured this was the least I could do.

18

Two weeks, one memory of hope

I will soon toot the Divorce Horn for the first time. This is not something I report to you with a sense of achievement or pride. But as I have committed to a full account of my break-up recovery plan, here goes nothing: it started in church.

If you are of the sort to be troubled by heresy, calm yourself, as there will be no sex in the transept. In fact I never entered the sacred part of the building at all. This story ends with me being finger-blasted by a young man behind a council rubbish bin—to be clear, some several metres away from God's house. But let me begin more earnestly and tell you what I had learned by that point about hope. This is for your own good.

It is not just during a break-up that you must be cautious with hope. It is at all times, such as twelve-step meetings and in health and sickness.

I have rarely been inclined to hope. This scepticism is one of the things I, a person of few good qualities, like best about myself. It was one of the qualities I liked best in my ex.

While it is true she was disposed to many moments of belief in semi-Hindu nonsense, especially in our final months, and was, if left unattended, a Truther who supposed there were things That They Don't Want You To Know, when it came down to the harder business of life, she could be marvellously averse to the garbage of hope.

I remember her warmly as she refused hope in the weeks after her diagnosis. Even when *I* didn't. I regret to report that I bought her a 'wellness' recipe book tailored by hopeful zealots to her disease. She opened it and said, 'If cheese is going to kill me then I don't want to fucking live,' and threw the volume across the room with the reminder that *I* was the one always going on about the loss of reason and the need to test hypotheses; remember when I made fun of Aunty Ida's acupuncture to her face?

'This thing has a *rainbow* on the cover. How could you?' she said to me. Quite right, too. There were no conclusive longitudinal studies about the impact of diet on her illness I could ever locate. This book was written not from reason but from hope.

I really had no business bringing the ideology of hope to a sick bed. She was correct. No one has any business doing this.

People do it, though. When things get tough, solutions can get really flimsy and the dying or seriously ill person not only has their pain and mortality to face but usually a long line of well-meaning tits like me all saying, 'I read something on the internet about bee-sting therapy and magnets. You should look into that.'

Even if few truly believe that pain can be treated with bone broth or a Tesla pendant, many believe in the medical power of hope. They believe that if a patient is not sufficiently 'positive' to believe in the possibility of a cure, however unlikely it is, then they are not prepared to live. It works if you work it, as I would hear them say at Al-Anon.

This is absolute bollocks, of course. Often nothing works at all.

The other patients on the neurology ward where she was diagnosed knew that positive thinking was bollocks too. When I said 'My girlfriend needs to be more positive!' to an elderly woman named Essie, who had suffered a serious spinal cord injury and was trapped inside a halo, she said, 'What in the name of ginger for?'

She made an excellent point. There is, to the best of my present knowledge, no evidence that a patient's positive attitude affects their prognosis.

Essie told me pain is just misery. It isn't, as it is often described, a 'battle', between the forces of hope and hopelessness, or one between a patient and disease. Pain is not a battle, it's a surrender.

'You wait. You see what happens. You let the people who seem to know what they are doing do things. That's it.'

No one has any therapy for a divorce better or more scientific than, say, going on one hundred dates within a year. There is no doctor, shaman or former alcoholic qualified to mend the pain of a break-up. You can't submit to treatment and, at one point or another, you're just going to have to agree to lie down and submit to defeat instead. Which is what the incurable Essie was finally compelled to do.

Essie told her niece who had come to visit that she did not wish to be described as having 'lost a battle' in the classifieds when she died. 'And don't say "passed away", either. "Dead" will do.' Her niece said, 'You're not going to die!' And while you and I are now agreed that truth is overhyped and modest lies can be polite, this was an untruth so extreme even the pathology nurse (who happened to be a fan of sexy vampire stories) rolled her eyes.

I bought the newspaper for some months after we left the ward. Eventually I saw Essie's name and read that she had 'passed away peacefully' having 'lost a battle'. Essie, who left this life in agony, had also lost the battle with her editorialising niece.

To insist that illness is a battle or that death is not the end rarely does service to the dying or the ill. These moments of hope serve only those of us in good health who do not care to see hope disappear. So I remain quite sorry that I bought my ex a wholefood recipe book with a rainbow on the cover. Actually, if she had left me for this dreadful excursion into hope, I could have understood it.

Hope had been an early sign that my ex was going to leave me. Hope, I have come to believe, is not a treatment for pain so much as it is a symptom of illness. Along with long hours spent at the gym, an unusual interest in Facebook and genitals that smell strongly of someone else, the suspicious spouse should watch out for hope. Hope was an irregular thing for her. Such a sustained period of it was unprecedented.

A few months before she left, the ex had joined a group of chanting simpletons whose goal it was to end the world's wars with 'positive thinking' and neurolinguistic programming, or similar gobshite. She became irritated when I offered the view that good vibes were no match for a good military.

She started listening to uplifting music whenever I tried to talk, which is often, so I heard a lot of kick drums and swooshing synths for about a year. Then, one afternoon, she painted the garage door a hopeful shade of orange, and when I asked if she wanted me to try to clean up the concrete that had been splashed orange, she said, 'No. I think random colour that lands where physics decrees is so beautiful. Don't *you*?'

Well, no, I fucking didn't. I don't like contrived boho design statements, I don't like giving up the security deposit on a rental house and, these days, and I don't much care for the colour orange.

Tuscany is full of orange, I hear.

I saw the crudely painted door and the rebellion its bright strokes strove to represent, and I began to see that something had shifted.

'Are you sleeping with Arty Sandra?' I had asked this tangerine stranger that day. She said no, she was just 'collaborating'. She said I had become a predictable thinker. I should *not* presume that a glorious orange door whose pigment was drawn into the driveway by the beating heart of the physical universe needed cleaning. I should *not* confuse a close artistic partnership with sex. Jeez, Helen. You're so bourgeois.

Bourgeois? This was certainly a case of the pot calling the kettle orange. There are few practices more ruling class than (a) adultery and (b) shabby-chic decorating.

I am not at all fond of cheating, but I am even less tolerant of a pseudo-design school that mimics the style of a down-on-its-luck upper class. Those who try to conceal their aspirations from themselves by dressing them in spattered paint and other signifiers of a faded wealth are, in my view, much more poisonous than those who simply buy pirated Burberry scarves. Pretending to be rich is far less offensive than pretending to be *formerly* rich.

Aspiration, the close cousin of hope, is a lie. An orange door is a lie. 'If I was sleeping with anyone else, I would tell you and we'd work it out' is a lie. And, yes, we all lie and the truth, a habit into which I'd fallen when she left, is often overvalued. But there's a fucking limit with the lies. I'm not too sure where it is, but you'll know it when you find it. It is somewhere close to hope.

Perhaps you will see your limit in a shabby-chic orange door whose imprecise edges, your soon-to-be-ex partner tells you, are testament to the lived glory of the universe, and the death of the bourgeoisie.

Perhaps by a hospital bed, where you'll find yourself exceeding the limit of reasonable lies. 'Everything will be okay,' you say. You're lying.

Hope is a lie. Hope doesn't work. Hope, to be clear, doesn't fix shit. And as much as the sex-destroying Karl Marx warned against it, apparently I still took the hope opiate now and then.

I believed that a three-way would save my marriage. I gave my ex a book of faith-based recipes when what she needed was a good neurologist. I had agreed to go to Al-Anon to Heal My Life when what my life needed was for me to look directly into its wounds and not to find plasters to conceal them.

I hate hope. Normally. Even more than I hate kale chips lightly toasted in cold-pressed natural oil. I *hate* it. I hate the hopeful farmers' market where I bought that stupid book. That week it was full, as it always is, of mothers loudly worrying if that lamb was raised on a diet rich in Omega 3; if that green smoothie was entirely biodynamic. Biodynamic is a made-up word that signifies nothing. 'Clean eating' is a harmful religious fiction. There can be no clean thing or fresh start in this world.

She would not eat the optimistic diet at the time of her diagnosis, but I would chow down on hope in my own critical hour. I would go to a meeting to tell my most shameful secrets to strangers and I would do this the same day I had allowed my home to be 'smudged'. Which was just a few weeks after

I had purchased a shamanic journey from a dude in Reykjavik and completely fallen for a few hundred text messages.

But I had been told several times that I 'needed to grow'. Which, you should be aware, is hopeful nonsense. People who have been newly dumped do not need to grow, as much as their departing spouses might valorise this goal for themselves. We don't need to grow. We need to go to bed and shrink right down to almost nothing so that one day we are small enough to rise.

If there was anything at all left to honour from our average years together, it was shared laughter at bullshit hope.

I readied myself for the first of twelve steps with the pamphlet Kay had given me. I took it and started towards a hopeful goal.

I would leave the hopeful pamphlet in a bin, not too far from a church, while I was impaled on an age-inappropriate finger.

19

Two weeks, one step, one moment by a bin that may be considered an indignity by some

The first step is pretty easy. It requires only the admissions that (a) one is 'powerless over alcohol' and (b) one's life 'had become unmanageable'.

I knew long ago that alcohol was something over which I had no control. And, of course, one look at either me or my bank balance would show how unmanageable my life had become. I had neither worked nor washed laundry in weeks. I had occasionally failed to piss exactly in the toilet. I was a bad life manager. The first step is easy.

The second step is not so straightforward. It requires that we nominate a 'Higher Power'.

Being of the view that life has no founding principle, I found this pretty tricky. 'I'm an atheist,' I said to Kay before we left the house. 'Actually, I'm a poly-non-theist, which is to say I don't believe in many gods.'

Kay, who *did* believe in a great many gods and angels, pretended to indulge my refusal to believe in some sort of Ultimate Purpose, but was really having none of it and who can blame her, as I had, after all, just permitted her access to every room in my house with a bouquet of burning weeds.

'Let's get you a higher power.'

I have since heard some adequate rationales for the function of this higher power by the otherwise faithless and recovering. They say it's important not to believe you have agency in all matters and this is good advice. There is stuff bigger than us. Of *course* there is. But in order not to believe that I have any real control, I don't see how I must believe in a force that has all of it.

Nonetheless, the twelve-steppers say you must believe in the power of something good in order to no longer submit to the power of things, and Kay advised me to just give up on the idea of a Karl Marx as god and perhaps nominate a tree in my yard as a higher power instead.

'Quick. Choose one. Go and say hello to it. Then we have to go.'

If you go to a Twelve Step meeting, and this is not always a terrible idea, you should know that the choice of a tree is stupid. Particularly a walnut tree and particularly one that has not been closely inspected for some months.

Although I am a keen gardener and it is my normal practice to look for signs of disease on all the plants with which I share a yard, I had been so busy looking for signs of disease in my relationship I'd failed to detect any elsewhere. So after a solemn moment of thinking about where a miserable atheist should locate her higher power, I made a decision and walked out the back to address it.

It didn't look well.

During months of suspicion and sadness, many of my higher power's branches had died, and those that had not were full of bleeding holes.

If you have a walnut tree that is discharging sap from multiple wounds, you probably have Thousand Cankers Disease. It's easy to identify but nearly impossible to cure. All you can do is cut back the dead wood and, um, hope. By no means should you nominate such a vulnerable plant as your higher power. It's a horticulturally unsound decision. Under a dying walnut tree, this village dickhead stands.

I didn't tell Kay that the tree was on the critical list. I figured I was stuck with it now and, in any case, we now needed to leave.

Kay had offered to drive me to a meeting we had selected online for its declared atheism and for its location in a suburb so distant I was unlikely to run into either God or anyone I knew. She offered to go in with me, too, and I understand that such fellowship is a good function of the twelve-step community, but I declined. I had completed few tasks more complex than pissing, crying and wanking, sometimes simultaneously, since the ex became the ex, and if I were to resume independent life better than the walnut tree this seemed like a good opportunity for a practice run.

Al-Anon is simple, and this is a good thing for people in distress. The rules are plain, the literature and meeting times are easy to find and the experienced twelve-steppers are sweet when a newbie who fumbles the words 'It works if you work it so work it 'cause you're worth it' takes a chair beside them.

Kay drove her Cherokee fast through progressively nicer suburbs. I made it in more than enough time. For a free-range earth-worshipping smudger, that bitch knows how to burn rubber.

I went in. I offered some coins to the collection plate and a sweet-looking man said no.

'You're new here. Welcome. Only give when you feel you have received.'

'Ha ha, I wish my ex had that attitude,' I said, thinly.

He didn't laugh but said, 'I know,' and made a steeple with his hands.

When the group began to 'share', I was struck for some minutes by the quality of speeches, which, for this meeting, had the second step as its focus.

'Let's talk about our relationship to our higher power.'

Mine had just died. Marvellous. I wondered what I might say, but shortly became too entranced by the others and I gave it no great further thought.

There were many clever atheists in this well-to-do suburb, most of which were describing much better than I could the hardship they'd encountered in the search for a god substitute.

THE HELEN 100

A young, beautiful and extravagantly gay man delivered a spontaneous eulogy for the death of his 'enabling' self. It was of a quality I could not have prepared, let alone extemporised. It was rich in rhythm and light in regret. This young man spoke of the simplicity of Al-Anon, including its slogan 'Keep it simple' with a complexity so poetic that I began to believe that regular attendance could truly Heal My Life.

Here was a man who had overcome the suicide of his alcoholic mother, a profound sense of guilt *and* the problem of god to emerge as eloquent and self-possessed. His speech was so fine my crude memory retained none of it. I only remember that it was compelling and largely concerned with the problem of the higher power.

The ladies were crying. The men were making steeples with their hands. I was staring at him in *utter disbelief* that my years of utter disbelief had thus far prevented me from coming to Al-Anon and hearing this and restoring all the painted orange lies in my life to disease-free, hardwood truth.

It was my turn to speak, and even though I wanted to be good I said something like 'The love is bleeding from my branches'. Which is the statement of a lunatic. But it was received with so much love, and I felt so much love for these people in return.

I had thought all the love I had given to my ex these past years in diminishing doses had just completely disappeared three days ago. I had thought that it was gone. But it seemed to return all at once and it had this healing, hopeful group as its object. And apparently they loved me back.

'I have Thousand Cankers Disease,' I said. 'I am a dying walnut tree.'

To the credit of the group and of the organisation whose behaviour it governed, nobody looked at me like I was a dick.

After I had 'shared' the problem of my diseased boughs, an older chap started on about how he angry he was with his higher power for not helping him get a better package at work.

'I've been doing all the affirmations,' he said. 'But I still haven't renegotiated my contract. When *is* it *my* time?'

When *will* it be Barbie's time to shine?

I told myself that a natural metaphor, however poorly explained, could not been nearly as gauche as admitting you expect to monetize your recovery. But they didn't look at him like he was a dick, either.

I was full of hope. Was hope so bad? I'm sure even Karl Marx had moments of hope; he must have, or would have otherwise fled the British Library screaming, 'Fuck you all, you don't deserve my help and work out a theory of value yourselves, you lazy wankers.'

Of *course* hope is shit. We know this. Karl knew this. And my Helen One Hundred was not based on hope but on probability.

This is how I reckon the whole thing to myself these days, anyway. *You* try doing something that stupid *and* not rationalising it afterwards. Even if my date plan was bullshit and even if hope *is* a sop, I still expect it to visit me briefly from time to time. But what I do not expect, nor long for, is to be quite so transported by the possibility of hope as I was in that meeting.

I was so hopeful. I would *definitely* come again. Perhaps even tomorrow. This was *great*. I could be on the seventh step by Tuesday. I left, hopeful. Feeling clean truth and love and the memory of impromptu speeches that spoke so well of loss.

I had not planned to say anything to anyone after the meeting, least of all to the abundantly homosexual and pretty young star, as it seemed to me that those who had come to be anonymous wished to remain so in the minutes post-adjournment. But he was walking to the same tram as me and when this became as plain to him as it had been for some metres to me, he smiled and said, 'Hey, Tree Disease!'

I smiled back. I explained how I had encountered difficulty in completing the second step. 'The thing is, my higher power was a walnut tree that turned out to be physically dead.'

I didn't mind being godless, I told him, but I was embarrassed about being a bad gardener. He laughed, and when told me that he despised the idea of god and even of a universal truth, I began to enjoy the conversation.

Intellectual arrogance has always been my default crime, but it had remained largely uncommitted living, as I had been for some time, in a death row of silence. So, I was responding to this young person as I normally don't. Which is with enthusiasm and appreciation, instead of impatience and opinions.

We talked about the problem of god and of locating any founding principle or final authority for life *like it was the first time.*

As I am a sceptic and a wanker in my forties, I had long ago thought my way into and then back out of meaninglessness. The questions of 'What does it all mean?' and 'Why are we here?' had been asked and answered to my ontological satisfaction. But for this young chap, who introduced himself to me as Hayden A, the transition into uncertainty was new.

For me, these thoughts were ancient. But they were also buried in years of writing cheap sales bullshit. These thought relics were sufficiently undisturbed that I had almost forgotten their original forms. So it almost felt new when he said, 'I think we just need to live with the idea that there is nothing.'

I responded first with genuine surprise that someone I had just met should say such an accurate thing and next with the vestiges of my knowledge on the matters of (a) nothingness and (b) not believing in everything.

It took a few minutes to find my shallow groove, but bits of anti-foundational thought borrowed from university came back to me in handfuls.

'Yes. The human world itself is will, and not much else! We are little more than a collection of drives! The only essence is the irremediable fact of no essence! The oceanic feeling of connection is nothing but a memory of infant life!'

These bits of Freud and Nietzsche and Sartre, and possibly Heidegger, who I'd never understood, were so badly remembered that they came out in an unrecognisable glob. It is therefore likely that they appeared to Hayden as my own ideas. I believe that it seemed to him that I had been so inspired by his anti-foundational thinking I was immediately doing some of my own.

There are few spectacles, I've heard, so seductive as the dying moments of someone else's innocence. This seeming death of my innocence—wow, this old chick finally sees that there is no purpose to life!—charged Hayden with a force of desire that was met, for other reasons, by me.

Then he said, 'I understand how much love you feel right now.' He tugged his infinity scarf for emphasis.

I understand how much love you feel right now.

Of all the things that were said to me about the nature of a break-up while I remained inside it, this remains the most insightful.

If you have felt the loss of a much-loved person, perhaps you know just how strong and fast love can surge when it finds itself alone. It's terrible to learn that your love continues to exist, even and especially without a responsive object. It's *obscene* to know that the love is just *there*. There it is: dumb and ugly and homeless. There it is: huge and present.

The thing about love is that it is just too large to fuck off in a hurry, if at all.

I understand how much love you feel right now.

Not many people are so foolish that they will say this wise thing. It's a great humiliation to admit that we can sometimes feel this big.

To say he understood how much love I felt, even with nothing to love, was to utter the sort of secret that is kept for very good reasons. As I'd been doing quite a lot of that myself lately, I felt exonerated. Someone else was doing the blurting for a change. He reminded me that our love is not something created for a special person. A special person is created by our love.

My special person had gone. But the love remained and had become unmanageable. In pointing this out, Hayden became my higher power. He said that he understood; having fallen into oceanic silence, I said nothing.

As I am not much of a drinker, there are few moments of mutually desired sexual activity in my life that have not been preceded by prattle. 'Would you mind if I kissed you?' or 'Could I possibly touch you there?' are the sorts of things I am wont to say, not only because I am a championship league talker but because I went to university in the nineties where it was very standard to utter contracts of sexual consent. 'Is it okay if I penetrate you gently?' became a routine first acquired from manuals prepared by the Women's Collective, and later maintained for my general love of talking.

On this occasion, however, there was no sex preamble and it might seem that I am the sort of cock about to tell you some malarkey like 'no words were necessary'. But words weren't actually necessary at all.

But before you begin, and not before time, to despise me, 'no words were necessary' does not necessarily describe a good thing. It doesn't mean that the desire was so intense and pure it transcends all attempts to describe it.

I can describe it. The stuff that was going on here wasn't very magical.

The fact was that Hayden A, impressive and independent as he was in speech, was just as susceptible to flattery as anyone. The sight of his own wisdom reflected in an older face really got to him. My face, acting as a mirror, compensated momentarily for my lack of a dick. What he saw was evidence of his own youthful force.

I think what I might have been guilty of here was confusing Hayden's youth for hope—even if he had been talking about the death of meaning. Perhaps that was my misapprehension. I'm not sure. It could have been the case that I was simply sick of masturbating. Also, he was a gorgeous little twink.

None of what I did with Hayden is terrible. Nor is it pathetic. It just happened to unfold next to a council rubbish bin. With a gay dude who was maybe twenty, twenty-one . . .

We led each other to the bin and gave ourselves over to vanity, rushing hope and silence.

Being well under 30, he had a very agile thumb and played me like an Xbox. Being well over 30, I had a great deal of gratitude so I played him like a horn. It was, in fact, the best and most thorough blozzer I had at that time ever offered to a gentleman and he thanked me for my end-to-end service. I *did* swallow after all.

After I had disposed of my pamphlet, bought one packet of sugar-free mints and one of moist towelettes from the 7-Eleven, we said a cordial goodbye.

Fifteen down. Eighty-five dates remaining.

I never returned to Al-Anon. This was partially due to my everyday pessimism, which had returned in full force when I was on my knees, post-climax, by a bin. It was also out of fear that I'd bump into Hayden, who probably felt bad not only for finger-banging an old dyke but that he'd done what they call in the program the 'thirteenth step', that is, getting off with a vulnerable newbie. He needn't have, though. His actions, in my view, were those of pure love, even if largely for the love of himself. Which was not a bad thing at all. He *was* very lovable.

But I mainly did not return to Al-Anon because I had got what I came for. It was not really the sex, which was adequate, that slightly improved me. It was that the entire evening was at once so foul and so sublime.

It was, and remains, very funny to think of myself being fingered by a precocious twink half my age, and at least one dress size smaller. It was very instructive to learn that a room full of strangers can produce real and mutual love for an hour at a time. It remains very moving to think that we can occasionally coincide with someone in our grief.

Hayden knew that my love was leaking all over the shop. That someone, or even a group of someones, was prepared, even for a bit, to absorb my love made the terrible fact of it seem much more manageable.

I can't say this exchange gave me much hope. I can say that it offered relief. I slept relatively well. I wouldn't have even bothered bathing before I blundered into bed, but did so as Eleven was so fascinated by my bin-smell I knew he would interrogate me with his snout all night.

If I could ever again face Kay, on whom I had bled so profusely, I would buy her a fifty-dollar entrée and tell her the story of how Al-Anon changed my life in just one evening.

If brief mutual love was possible, then perhaps a more sustained sort was, too. Al-Anon gave me faith that Helen One Hundred was not a totally shit idea.

20

Three weeks, incalculable texts

By the next Sunday, I saw that the Helen One Hundred was a totally shit idea.

First, that callous, narcissistic, faithless tit John hadn't contacted me in days. Or, perhaps, a day. *Yes*, I had told him some malarkey about how I was 'busy' with 'work' 'all month'. But this should not have prevented him from ignoring me and claiming all my time for himself. That he had not been driven for almost an *entire day* to contact my Very Fucking Special self in a colossal fit of passion was a sure sign of masculine weakness. I hoped he was enduring a wholesome menu and dreary sacred sex with Arachnia, the baby-killing doula.

Second, I had online dating interaction that morning of a quality typified by a chap called 9_2_make_u_cum.

'hi ladies,' he wrote, 'i got 9 2 make u cum.'

On the Lord's day!

My concerns about this message, and its author, were several. After spending three days on the sex internet, I had learned to forgive many errors of expression, including a lack of capitalisation (although I still wasn't tolerant of *unnecessary* capitalisation, particularly when applied to any Lesbian who was not Sappho herself). However, the fact that I had been pluralised was a worry, in both a grammatical and a psychological sense. *Ladies*.

An introductory message that simply restated the obvious promise of its author's username also seemed a bit bonkers. Furthermore, I have a fairly shallow vagina and no real capacity for '9'.

With no notion how to proceed after such an introduction I simply typed: 'Really?'

'Fo sho,' came the reply. This claim was supported by a picture of the 9, alongside a subscription-television remote control, whose length it slightly exceeded.

9_2_make_u_cum: yo check ur foxtel remote im bigga

MidLifeISIS: I thank you for your interest in (a) my multiple selves and (b) the eager promotion of Rupert Murdoch's entertainment distribution empire. He surely needs the boost. I, or we, regret that as I have the option of banging myself up the arse with a napkin ring—and it is one of fairly good quality that I bought from a reputable online vendor—I am not at current liberty to meet a fine fellow like you. If things don't work out with the dinnerware or a catastrophic event befalls the earth and we have the only two sets of intact mammal genitals within it *and* I've misplaced this napkin ring and all those others in my collection, I'll certainly be in touch. Otherwise, I wish you all the best with your television viewing, whose wireless operation I hope is not clogged by semen. Can't have you missing Downton.

Then I texted Celine, whom I knew was a Foxtel subscriber, to make sure that the for-scale remote was around nine inches. I also wanted to let her know there was an online person called 9_2_make_u_cum, which I knew she'd find funny.

Celine: Nine to make you come!!!!!!

Celine: Could I possibly get his phone number?

A few minutes later, my friend replied again with a picture of her own Foxtel remote device set next to a tape measure. It was 20.5 centimetres, which, upon consulting Google, we learned was just over eight inches in the old money, thereby legitimising the claims made by 9_2_make_u_cum.

Australia has long been a very metric nation. Yet the inch unit had persisted with my age-mates for the measurement of cock. I asked Celine, who is more than a decade younger than me, if imperial was still used to evaluate those penises in her age-range.

Celine: Yep. Dudes my age use inches as well. Not sure why. Perhaps it makes it easier for them to extend the truth?

Celine: Nobody even sends me dick pics anymore. How do I even live?

And then she called, which Millennials rarely do. She had an idea that she found Very Exciting.

At a library not too far from my home, there was that night to be an event known as Literary Speed Dating. This was bound by the rules of regular nineties speed dating: basically a case of matchmaking musical chairs but with added intellectual elitism.

'I know you're usually too much of a snob to deign to mix it with other snobs,' said Celine. 'But considering that all you've got so far is a few big words from some shadowy manboy, possible syphilis of the throat and a huge library of dick pics, you might want to give it a try.'

Literary Speed Dating demands that each participant brings their favourite novel. Few of those people sufficiently insecure to attend an event with the word 'literary' in its title, of course, would bring their *favourite* novel. We'd all bring our most self-verifying novel; the thing with which we wanted to be identified, not necessarily the thing that we loved.

My favourite novel, or at least the one that has brought me the most pleasure, is *Carry on, Jeeves*. It's hilarious. I would not, however, want it put about that valet Jeeves is my fictional hero or, by Jove, that I secretly adore Wooster, who is such an oofy cove. People might think me a protector of cruel class structures, which is not the case. If I was in favour of any kind of hierarchy, it was only that of literary taste. Which, as it turned out, P.G. Wodehouse was too. 'There is no surer foundation for a beautiful friendship than a mutual taste in literature,' he is alleged to have once said.

This quote, with which I agreed despite knowing that I should not, was written on the Facebook event page. So, in this case, anything by Wodehouse was definitely too obvious.

I wondered about a subtler title.

The terrible truth was that I had given up on novels a few years back—about the time I started being conscientiously miserable. Fiction is a pleasure obtainable only by those who do not hate their own lives so much they are unable to consume idealised accounts of others'. As such, I had long been on an unhappy diet of Marxist nonfiction or senseless marketing briefs.

The only novel I had read in about a decade was *Fifty Shades of Grey*. Which I have read often as I really liked taking the piss out of it, particularly with Celine, who attributed to E.L. James a partial cure for her major depressive illness on account of this author being so very, very funny.

Over a year, Celine and I must have texted each other all of the sentences from that unintentionally camp book at least twice. A few months after the book's publication, and days after I had attempted to use it for wanking, I began sending Celine passages from it and she began to send them right back. We had both been unhappy for different reasons and became mutually dependent on this exchange for some time. So when she didn't send me at least one per day, I knew that she was suffering a serious depressive episode and would immediately call her sister. Otherwise, it was a regular trade of:

He's my very own Christian Grey popsicle.

Or:

My inner goddess is doing the dance of the seven veils.

Or, my favourite:

His voice is warm and husky like dark melted chocolate fudge caramel . . . or something.

This last one always buoyed my confidence as a writer.

I supposed that I could take *Fifty Shades*, cock my head, bite my lip ('I'd like to bite that lip, Anastasia Steele!') and talk about my Inner Goddess all evening until someone got the joke that Celine and I had so ardently overworked.

But piss-taking wasn't likely to be a good romantic tactic outside of my currently paused 'relationship' with manboy John. If I wanted to progress beyond being mouth-fucked by a gay teenager next to a bin, I probably needed to play nice.

I needed a novel that said something clear and palatable about me to fifteen male persons with whom I'd endure two minutes of 'literary' conversation.

'I am trying to find a novel on my shelf that represents me, HALP!' I texted Celine about as soon as I'd hung up.

She replied, 'Don't you dare bring *The Bell Jar*.' Which is good general advice, but was no immediate help at all.

'Just find some writing that means almost nothing to anyone,' she wrote next. Which is actually the advice that brings success to the best commercial copywriters. Before she had an epiphany/serious depressive episode, Celine was paid much more handsomely than I ever was to do this sort of work. She was, when she was unwell, good at saying nothing. She had said to me once or twice that she wished, now that she was well, that everything wasn't so *meaningful*.

Writing without meaning is a tall order. Unfortunately, the newly dumped infer *every* meaning from *every* word. Thanks to John, I had recently discovered about 70 new meanings for the phrase 'Hi Helen'. So, given that there was nothing I would *not* find meaningful, I considered bringing an actual favourite from the shelf.

My favourite novel at university had been Shelley's *Frankenstein*. Probably not a good idea. This book, reasonably considered the foundational work of science fiction, could send a beckoning signal to an Arthur C. Clarke nerd—no diss to the sci-fi faithful, but I just wasn't up to any person who believed in the future.

Frankenstein might also cause persons to think me dark. Not dark like the desire pooled in the sexy loins of Anastasia Steele, but, you know, darkly depressed.

I didn't need any help on that count. I was already darker than the dark shadow of a miserable Promethean monster drowned in a cup of Starbucks' darkest roast. One with no milk, served during a midnight power failure in Christian Grey's dungeon at a moment of lunar eclipse. So, it was a no to Mary Shelley, who would either illuminate or darken me falsely.

I remembered that the last novelist I'd gone truly mad for was Jeanette Winterson, but as this was not a lesbian event, such a declaration could only advance my loneliness. Or, possibly, set me up with the lady librarian. Which *was* a thought.

I've always fancied lady librarians.

Who hasn't?

I'm sure that lady librarians, who are universally suspected of exquisite perversion, are all already taken. Probably taken polyamorously. Whatever the case, no easy bet like *Oranges Are Not the Only Fruit* would tempt these hotties from their sexually and textually rich lifestyles.

I still didn't know what to bring, and Eleven, never a keen student of literature, was unhelpful on this count.

It was a bit of a shock, as a former serious scholar of English, to find that I had lost the knack for literary criticism. I just didn't know what would fly. I decided to make a list of books from my shelf *not* to bring. I started with Sylvia Plath, as per Celine's advice, and moved on to Jodi Picoult.

I hadn't purchased this Picoult book but had stolen it in a moment of literary activism. I had come across it when a client had dispatched me to a health retreat for five days; I was there to write some uplifting detox copy. If I overlooked all the yin, yang and Healing Power of Herbs, I had a decent time. I lost three kilos and enjoyed two colonic treatments.

Now I am a fan of both losing weight and sticking things in my arse, but I wasn't a fan of the fat-farm library, which was dreadful. As there was no 'toxifying' television in the resort, I was forced to read a Jodi Picoult novel. (It was either that or a book on shamanism.) I had liked it only slightly more than *Fifty Shades of Grey* and even a little less than my teleconference with an 'actual' shaman. Which is still not an incident I can talk about.

Anyhow, I had stolen the book to prevent others from reading it. Don't ask me why I found it so offensive. It's probably just because I am vile and I dislike women who can feel things.

Eventually, I went with *Anna Karenina*. Don't hate me. Or do. In either case, please know I will continue to hate myself so consummately, you needn't even bother. And in news that will be unsurprising to anyone who can spell the word 'book', I was not the only chick holding Anna that night. She's the literary equivalent of a white button-down shirt. Everyone believes they will look good with this staple. Hardly anybody does.

But it could have been worse. I could have gone with *Catch 22*, which about half the chaps had. What is this supposed to say about a suitor? Either, 'I'm a complex and self-consciously disturbed person who believes he can see the true nature of things better than you', or 'I haven't heard that intellectually conceited white boys are supposed to carry 'round *Infinite Jest* yet.'

This was the first library I'd visited in years. The cheap nature of my work had rarely led me to them, and even though I had enjoyed libraries at one time, I had long since given up doing anything that I enjoyed. But I had, in extreme youth, spent enough time in libraries to feel comfortable in one again now.

Libraries hadn't changed much. Even though there were fewer shelves and many more PC terminals and children's discovery areas than in those libraries of my memory, this one smelled just the same. You know that smell. That not entirely unpleasant flesh-mildew smell with top notes of compost. Whatever that library smell is, apparently technology hadn't yet delivered its antidote.

There was a lady at a central table who looked very much like BDSM Odette. Same lavish silhouette, same snarl and similar magenta-coloured hair. It made perfect sense that this was the style of the modern librarian: a sexy, curvy dom with a good 'do and little patience.

'All book sluts report to me!' she cried, and I checked to make sure this wasn't, in fact, Odette.

I gave the hot librarian five dollars and took a name tag and began to fill it in. Libre-dom said, 'Not so fast, Sunshine, the librarian keeps the records around here,' and she asked me my name so she could write it in her fair and consistent hand.

I began to say the word 'MidLifeISIS', but managed to stop myself before the first syllable was done.

'Sorry?' said la fetishista.

'Um. Mi. Min. My name is Minnie.'

Who the fuck is called Minnie, other than a well-known mouse and a single quirky human entertainer about once every fifty years? Minnie sounded like a fake name, so I was not surprised a bit when Catwoman handed the name tag back and said, 'O-kay *Minnie*. Enjoy a night honestly and openly connecting with others as your*self, Minnie*.'

My name may not have been Minnie, but I *had* actually read the book that I was holding, so I wasn't bullshitting about that. I'd read it some years ago, but I'd topped up with a bit of an audio recording before my arrival. As I listened I was struck by how much Tolstoy had improved in the twenty years I'd left him on his own. It had finally become a great book. Good work, Leo.

Perhaps owing to my recent revival of interest in Marx, *Anna* had become a pre-revolutionary Russian tale. I was surprised that I had always thought of it as the exquisitely written love story of two insufferable fuckwits. This time, and from the outset, I could tell that all the princes and princesses sniffed the imminent loss of their comforts. You can sense it in the movement of the Moscow trains. Vronsky and Anna seemed to matter a lot less this time. The railway worker that Anna sees crushed to death in the moment she meets the Count is as important to the text as she is.

While I was cribbing, I saw that Trotsky had eulogised Tolstoy in 1910. 'Tolstoy did not know or show the way out of the hell of bourgeois culture,' wrote Leon, but he had depicted it with irresistible force. Trotsky then went on to write that *he* happened to know the way out of bourgeois hell and, no, it did not involve painting the doors of Moscow a rustic orange. The answer was 'scientific socialism'.

I would try not to mention this. I would try not to screw myself.

Actually, it didn't seem as though I could screw myself that evening. When Cruella de Book rang the bell to signal the first two-minute Speed Dating conversation, hardly anyone but me was speaking at all.

Being capable of emitting any kind of full sentence about anything at all, even socialism, gave me a head start. Perhaps the people who attend five-dollar Literary Speed Dating at local libraries are the kinds of people even *more* socially anxious than me. I guess that means I can unenthusiastically propose that the just-dumped dater try it.

I found myself, for the first time in some time, to be the life of the party, and I don't mind telling you that it felt rather fine. Right up to the point that I realised that shy people are most comfortable with other shy people.

On my right, there was a young woman with a handsome, heavy brow. She had liquorice hair, big tits and a tiny body. She had the sort of complexion you just knew had never been touched by make-up and we probably shouldn't be surprised that she was holding *Twilight*. The chap who sat before her was a good twenty years her senior, which put him at about my age. He was holding something that looked a bit sword-and-sorcery and the two were getting along as famously as people who find it painful to speak can. I could see their mutual May–September interest and instantly disapproved of it and of him in particular, until I remembered that I'd slid up and down a finger of someone younger than Bella just a week ago.

To my left, a sci-fi man was blushing at a sweet-looking lass of, I'd say, thirty-two. I saw he had *Neuromancer*, which I'd actually read and even liked. She had Jodi Picoult. The one about cancer I'd stolen from the fat-farm, I think.

Gragan, the chap with horn-rimmed glasses who first sat in front of me, wasn't much younger than me, but I sensed he needed to believe that he was. 'If you show me yours, et cetera!' I said, presenting my book like a game show model and offering the nicest kind of smile that I could.

'Um, you've probably never heard of it.'

'You've probably never heard of it' is the maxim of hipsters. I do not like hipsters. They are a group of wilfully heedless tits that hold fast to the fiction that they got first to wherever it is they think that they're at. Which is the place that you are, necessarily, not. Hipsters tend to define themselves by imaging the stupidity of others.

It's not that I mind a little arrogance, a little battle-of-the-snobs. Actually, I love it, and I have for all my life challenged people to prove that they know more or less than I do. But I don't go about pretending that the world has no memory or history—'you've probably never heard of it' should never be one's first assumption. Hipsters, I have found, are criminally ahistorical. You can see this in the way that they dress: beat poet with some sort of fifties-inspired normcore with a hint of a Socialist Alternative activist c. 1984.

Horn-rim's book, by the by, was *A Confederacy of Dunces*. I'd heard of it, but politely pretended that I never had. I was super nice to Gragan, which I find is always easy when you dislike someone that much at first sight.

I used all of the skills acquired in a professional life of interviewing, and I flattered him for two minutes with my interest. 'What do *you* think?', 'What's *your* opinion?', 'How do *you* feel about that?' Basically, all the crap you learn working in advertising media: use the second-person pronoun a lot. Pretend that you really fucking care.

He asked me nothing about myself, or my Tolstoy book, which was fine by me. I could never be honest with someone likely to say 'you've probably never heard of it'. I could never touch someone frightened of their age, which was the same as my age; someone so frightened of history.

I met three *Catch 22*s, four sci-fi/fantasy books whose details did not compute, *Neuromancer*, who was sure to get cosy with another Anna, one Franzen, one Crichton and a *Hunger Games*.

Toward the end, a handsome chap in a Breton shirt plopped, quite impatiently, before me and said, 'Look, this really isn't going well.'

Thank goodness.

He was called Javeer. He looked, maybe, West Asian. He had a big nose, which I like a great deal, but not half as much as I like the posture of a man who has just emptied himself of hope.

'No, Javeer. It's not going well. It's a terrible sham and I haven't read this book for twenty years.'

'I haven't read mine at all,' said Javeer.

He had a library copy of Graham Greene's *Brighton Rock*, which, as I told him, was a chic decision.

'I pulled it off a shelf,' said Javeer. 'Complete accident. I wish I could say the same for my presence, but obviously I was hardly brought here at gunpoint. Anyhow, you've got thirty seconds. Then I'll have thirty seconds. In that time, we'll say the most potentially alienating things about ourselves that we possibly can. Let's not repeat the mistakes of history. You know what they say, first as tragedy, then as farce. It'll save time and unnecessary optimism. All our faults. Go. *Go!*'

'Um. Right. I. Am. I. I am newly dumped from a same-sex relationship whose dreary background of infidelity and illness is something I fear I shan't escape for years. I am a boring, not very scholarly communist who often gets basic communist things wrong. Thanks for the Marx quote, incidentally. I recently went down on a young gay man after a twelve-step meeting. I swallowed. It was by a bin and I can still smell the garbage on my jeans because I'm so depressed these days I can't do my laundry. I quit my job. I'm broke. I believe my cat to be the only being I have ever truly loved. I possibly like being beaten.'

'Well done,' said Javeer. 'I am Zoroastrian, which probably sounds so exotic to you and I can tell you're the sort who would just love that. I can hear you now, you pretentious sow, "Oh, yes. My new boyfriend Javeer. He's Zoroastrian, you know." I'm also quite brown, which I feel needs to be said out loud in these ultra-white conditions. I, too, have dabbled in the homosexualist arts. As recently as this morning, in fact. I actually quite like women, but I don't think I could ever love one meaningfully. I do, however, have a passionate attachment to my emotionally violent mother who would probably rather eat glass than see me remain unmarried. There's about ten Parsi women in Australia, so she has learned not to care if the wife is white. Neither do I. I am looking for a possibly white wife respectable enough to match my high income, Minnie.'

'Oh,' I said. 'There's another thing. When I was giving the ring mistress my name, I started to say the one I use for my internet sex chat. But it came out as Minnie. My name is Helen. My name is Helen, and I'm an internet sex addict.'

'Well. My name is Javeer and I have Grindr active this minute. Where I may go by the username The Arse Whisperer. What is your nickname, incidentally?'

'Oh, look, I thought MidLifeISIS would be funny at the time.'

It was pretty good, he said, and we agreed that we would leave arm-in-arm as soon as the event was done and not wait about for the post-match niceties. We would only separate when we were a safe distance from the library and let Snitty McWhip believe that she had heard the painful blow from cupid's dart. After that, he said he'd attend to Grindr business. I said sure, and that I'd return home to masturbate to old messages from John.

We exited together after the last bell.

'I like you,' I said. 'I think we should stay in touch.'

'I like you, too,' he said. 'But, sweetie, I'm a time-poor arse whisperer looking for a convenient beard. Preferably one with a job and a hairdo of which my mother would approve. And you're such a divorced, unemployed fuck-up, you're not even *fake* marriage material. Next!'

That was another, what, twelve? Oh, fuck it. Let's call it fifteen. Thirty dates down. Just another seventy humiliations to follow.

21

Three, maybe four weeks, another decalitre of tears
For some time I considered Javeer's remarks. He was right. I was a mess, and not an appealing madcap sexy one at all. Of course, if his critique had not been delivered at the irresistible speed of camp, I would never have listened. But classical Gay has a knack for transforming even the mortal insult into a greeting, which is the opposite of the violence done to words by the Scottish tongue.

One late summer weeknight, I met a Scot who made 'Pleased to meet you' sound like a threat of death. She was a funny Glaswegian butch I'd met on the internet.

On the app, this lady had described herself as a 'chapstick lesbian', which I thought was good. Her username was Anne_Thrax, which was also rather good. When I met her in a tapas joint, I said that her gruff messages were the best I'd found on the Sapphic internet. She replied, 'Och. We Caledonians do make a good fist of it. If you catch my brackish drift from the River Tay, lassie.'

I hoped this handsome woman would do me. I enjoyed her comedy and her butch Scottish theatrics, and I was *almost* a femme.

Until I remembered that I was also such a divorced, unemployed near-femme fuck-up, and a girl-on-girl fisting could well be the sort of thing that would send me to the emergency room. I was possibly too fragile for rough sex, and certainly too familiar with the local hospital to flirt with the possibility of a return. They knew me there only as a brave and tearful wife. If I could, I would prefer to live in the memories of the medical staff as a sensitive and devoted partner, not remembered in hospital records as 'reckless whore with bleeding muff inexplicably tied up in tartan'.

Not, mind, that I ended up with a choice to be brutalised. After just two dishes, Anne_Thrax put her finger through a garlic squid ring and said, 'Aye, you're not my type.'

Thirty-one down. Sweet 69 to go.

Back home, I asked Eleven what I might do. He advised that I lay in one place and cry quietly for a week, just as soon as I'd filled his bowl with sashimi-grade salmon. 'No, Prince Puffy Pantaloons,' I said. Instead, I brushed his pelt for a bit and admired the spots on his tummy.

I have seen no display more mesmerising than that of a wallowing tabby. A loving, fat and happy cat can rotate his breadth around a brush without appearing to act on the matter at all. I could *never* tell how he flopped so quickly from spotty recumbence onto his paws without a *trace* of internal strain. Of course, all of my questions to him about his feline biomechanics had remained unanswered for years. Tabbies never tell. I supposed these cat gymnastics had something to do with spinal torque. I knew that they were always mysteriously good.

People who do not know cats well suspect they are inscrutable. People who do know cats well are certain of it. The more you love a cat, the better you learn that he is a riddle, wrapped in a mystery, inside a stripy coat. He is one of zoology's puzzles and has never told the secrets of his movements or his purr. Or of his mystery love.

Nearly every day, Eleven jumped up to lay on my desk. Between his naps, he would look at me as I worked. It's a look rare to any species. I'd never seen it on any other face, and I doubted that I would.

That was until Ameera, who is no particular confidante of cats, told me an Islamic folktale.

I had been at the desk months ago when Ameera called, and then said that she couldn't hear me properly. I said that Eleven was asleep on my mouse-operating arm, and that the poor sound was the likely result of my bungling lefty.

'Well, move the cat and use your right hand for the phone,' she said.

'But he really looks so happy. I'm going to leave him there.'

'Well, at least you have one thing in common with Mohammed,' she said. 'Peace be upon him.'

The story goes that the Prophet was readying himself for the call to prayer. He saw that his cat, Muezza, was snoozing on the sleeve of his prayer robe. Rather than disturb the cat, Mohammed used a pair of scissors to cut away the fabric. He heeded the call sleeveless.

There is a similar story, Ameera said, about a Sufi mystic. When asked why he would have done such a thing to his robe for a cat, he answered, 'Nothing changed.' Which is just the sort of enigmatic thing Sufis are wont to say.

I am by no means the spiritual type, but I love this folktale. And I like that Islam, and other religions, can brook a little of the mystery that is not even explained by God. A secular life has just as many enduring mysteries as a religious one, but we atheists are in the habit of looking for answers nonetheless. Sometimes you should just let the cat ruin your holiest clothes. A pause for love is sometimes *that* important. Cut the robe. Respect the mystery. Don't think science or God can explain it.

When Ameera told me this story, which I have since learned devout cat ladies of the world already know by heart, I began to consider the terrible possibility that some *people* gazed at each other in the loving, mysterious way my cat and I did.

This *must* have been what the story conveyed.

I can't imagine that a prophet or a mystic or anyone in the eternity business confines their earthly love to cats. The cat is clearly a metaphor. Old tales about animals don't generally survive if they teach us only about animals. I supposed this was a story about the nature of love and a reminder that it is a mystery for which one makes mysterious sacrifice.

Sacrifice, and you will be loved.

There is probably some Hadith or other that explains the mystery of love. But as I have indicated, my reading had been limited for years. Just Karl Marx and marketing documents. More recently, it had been pamphlets prepared by the twelve-step community or genuinely perplexing offers of fake-rape from the internet.

And text messages.

John: We can only suppose that yours is a life of such organised empowerment as you have not been in touch. Oh, the Woman Who Has It All. How DOES she juggle the demands of the boardroom and the bedroom?! How DOES she Lean In while retaining Pilates posture? How DOES she find time to meet a male companion of mild productivity and only modest looks? No one knows how she does it, day after day. But, they know that she does. And will, at 7 p.m. tomorrow. Let's meet at Richmond station.

'Could he ever look at me like you do?' I asked Eleven.

He said it depended on the quality of the salmon.

22

Four weeks, I think, dangerous volume of poetry
>When I am with you, we stay up all night.
>When you're not here, I can't go to sleep.
>Praise God for those two insomnias!
>And the difference between them.

This is from Rumi, the Sufi mystic we all know best. I do not know if he is the guy who honoured cats. I do think we can all agree he is much better than Coldplay.

We can probably also agree that following a Rumi reference, this story will now be every bit as suspenseful to you as the matter of next week's banking hours as upon meeting him, I became sleeplessly obsessed with John.

To be fair, the prick was reasonably handsome. He was also reasonably tall. It was a warm night, so when I was close enough to him to shake his hand I could smell him. It wasn't a bad smell—certainly, it was better than kitty litter. But it wasn't a great one, either. It was not that he had not bathed—I believe he had. It was just that this particular smell coincided with my old idea of a working man.

I would later describe his smell in my appalling blog as 'butterscotch and tobacco'. Clearly, I was trying to get a job as a Starbucks copywriter that day. In actual fact, he smelled more like sausages cooking in a pub. Maybe some graphite as well. He smelled like working men had largely ceased to and I felt myself drawn to him not only because he was attached to a penis that was still sober at 7 p.m., despite my fears derived from his many drunk dispatches by text late at night. I probably wanted to be close to him so I could sniff some of the buried memories I had of men.

Many men in my fashionable town assume a seventies style. They claim to be passionate about the football and they wear retro-kitsch cologne. They drive obscene old cars from which they ironically blare their yacht rock. They wear club colours on top of their bespoke western shirts, and even though some of them are slightly hipster I quite like the way they play with the symbols of a dying patriarchy.

When first I saw him on Platform 5, I thought that John was one of these fun mock-masculine men. Then I smelled him and started to believe that he wasn't impersonating an old-fashioned lad. He actually *was* one. He was real.

Public Service Announcement: Quite soon after that shithead has left you, you will meet somebody who you will believe to be 'authentic'. Now, I'm not saying that this person you find so beguiling is particularly inauthentic. But I am saying *please*, for the sake of blind shit, stop being so convinced that there is anything *authentic* out there at all. Authentic, if you ask me, is an inauthentic concept. It's also one likely to preoccupy you at a time when you don't know truth from lies. Just give up on this. You will *never* know truth from lies. You may learn, when the divorce dust settles, to recognise lies. But the verifiable existence of these lies is no proof at all of a reliable truth. So stop telling yourself that the truth is right there before you. Even if it smells good to you. Even if you have encountered it in a very authentic place, such as a public transit hub. And it is wearing a becomingly unfashionable short-sleeved business shirt.

On the platform, I learned that John was from the country and that he carried a mechanical pencil in his pocket. Google had already told me that he worked for the nation's oldest political party, but not that he was inclined to use phrases like 'the bosses and the workers' without actually taking the piss.

I knew from our messages that he had moderate cultural literacy and so must have understood that so much of what he seemed to be to others was antique. *Some* of this vintage shop steward stuff must have been a conscious act. But I was prepared to believe that some of it was also due to a genuine loathing for our era. This was a cause I could certainly support.

When he made a brief crack about that day's prime ministerial address, I knew he was not hopeful. When he walked toward me, I knew he was not my height. When he stood beside me, I knew that he smelled like my very old memories of a man.

Tall. Male. Documented interest in federal politics and none whatsoever in hope. These qualities provided such sufficient distance from my ex that I immediately wished to be close to them.

As I suspect many newly dumped people are, I was also quite conscious of those differences and how they drove me. I'm sure there are folks just dumped by a garrulous man who now find themselves attracted to a quiet one. I'm sure there are those who have been kicked in the 'nads by a large-breasted woman and now long to hold an A-cup in their hand. I wanted difference. I saw that he provided it.

What I failed to see then, even as I looked into two familiar brown eyes, is that, physically, he could have been her brother.

'It's a lovely night,' I said.

'Sorry, but I'm not quite sure what we do now,' said John.

'Well, didn't we say we'd decide when we got here?'

'Oh. We did. Sorry.'

I was getting a bit shitty, so I said, 'Are you sorry that you forgot, or do you mean that you are sorry that you are currently uncertain, or are you just finding this entire situation sorry?'

'Um. Columns A through C. Sorry.'

'Look, if you want to leave, that's okay,' I said, even though I knew that such a rejection would lead me to a barbecue chicken relapse.

'Sorry,' said John. 'I'm sorry.' And he just ruddy stood there.

When others fall into difficult doubt, I have the bad habit of becoming brutally certain. When they fall into complicated silence, I talk and act as boldly as I can.

So I said, 'It is clear that you are sorry. It is not so clear what you are sorry about. I can only suppose that I am, being the only person to whom you are currently addressed, the source for all this *sorry*. As I neither have wish to hear further apologies nor cause you to produce them, I will now take my leave. We can't have you feeling so sorry.'

'Sorry,' he said.

Oh, for the *sake* of fizzy drinks.

There was nothing for it now but to return home via Platform 7 and prepare for a life in poultry. I'd start calling the chicken man again. I'd marry the chicken man, if he'd still have me.

I was terribly embarrassed by this sorry rejection, but I had been told that such ignominy was common. It is usual, I had heard, for internet dates to end in minutes. Or for internet relationships to die when they move to real life within days.

Celine had warned me that the speed of the technology has come to shape the speed of the real. 'Look, Grandma. Don't expect courtly love from this manboy,' she had said to me that day by Skype, which I had used to showcase a range of different date looks. 'If he finds he doesn't click with you as fast as a cursor, he might fuck right off back to fuckstick land. In my experience, some of them do.'

Although John remained quite still, looking down at his unfashionable shoes, I was sure that he was passively fucking off.

Of course I found it painful to compare the sunny nature of our messages with the sorry nature of our meeting. But I was now adapted enough to pain to walk right through it.

'Bye,' I said, and I began to move away.

And he said, 'No, sorry. You have this all wrong,' and there followed a dreary exchange in which he said sorry for being so sorry and sorry again, and I demanded copious reassurance that he was not just sorry that my virtual appearance was not matched by my sorry physical one, and he said something like, 'No, it was exceeded,' then dropped his voice to a lower register and asked, please, if he could take me to his local around the corner.

I said that I would feel more comfortable closer to my home and I said this not because I really cared where I was one jot. I just wanted to get on a fucking train because, in the past few minutes, I had become envious of commuters. They had moved forward with such certainty while I fell back into sadness.

So we boarded a train.

I looked at him. For a minute or so, I feared that bird-watching, compulsively apologising, poorly dressed John was not, in fact, someone with an appealing dash of neurodevelopmental disorder but a full-blown nutter. A nutter, I had noted as I sat beside him on the train, that clearly lifted weights.

I understand that the 40-something chap may be directed by his doctor to lift weights. However, John, who was a smoker and a drinker and obviously a frequent sausage eater, didn't seem the sort to heed medical advice. Nor did he seem, in his hideous shirt, like the sort who cared much for his appearance. Therefore, even knowing that I was much more likely to be butchered by my statistical husband than by this awkward stranger, I had to consider that those guns had been developed not for reasons of vanity or health but with only femicide in mind.

John was an outlier. I was his improbable victim. The thought of death troubled me more now than it had a few nights previous as I worried that if I were slaughtered outside of my home, Eleven would have no meat.

These, I regret to report, were the thoughts in my actual head, and while they were quite unpleasant to endure they did help me achieve two good outcomes, and a third whose goodness I am yet to assess.

First, I was forced to address the gory and unreasoned nature of my thinking while in a public place. It is easy to think about being killed and then eaten by one's cat while in a private misery. It is only when these post-divorce thoughts occur to you in the company of others that you come to see that you have been completely off your rocker. I truly recognised that I was bonkers, in a way that not even Javeer had conveyed.

I was bonkers, but no longer so bonkers that I refused to see it as a problem. Good outcome.

Second, I was relatively quiet during this period of minor catharsis. This got John talking. A little about his day, a little about the social anxiety that prompted him to say sorry so much, and quite a bit about the European Central Bank. Which I found interesting and knew would be useful information when I saw Eleni next. She had strong opinions on the Greek debt crisis. Good outcome.

Third, I had decided that we would go to my place, because I had shut up for long enough to see that he probably wasn't going to murder me with those questionable muscles. I still don't know if we can call what followed a good outcome.

The walk home was pleasant enough and dominated by discussion of John Maynard Keynes. The evening was tolerably warm and I was not murdered.

Then a very pretty Burmese rubbed against John's legs as we were about to cross a busy road. When it seemed to me as though the cat was about to throw itself under traffic, I shouted, 'NO! John! Stop the puss!' and he dutifully did.

He held the cat and the cat started purring. I am sure I have no need here to report the arousing effects of this action. As we have learned, some women are won by male demonstrations of paternal concern. Whereas I will fuck just about anyone that is nice to a cat.

John, who was an online dater of some years' dedication, had likely met many childless cat ladies before. Perhaps he'd mastered some trick of feline hypnotism known only to a sensitive sub-branch of pickup artists.

Public Service Announcement for Heterosexual Midlife Men: Greatly increase your chances of finding pussy by learning to love the domestic cat.

The cat, he said, as he turned it on its back to look at its collar, was a female called Champers, presumably a diminutive for Champagne. He said that there was a phone number and that he should probably call it.

At this point, John could have asked his entire football team around for a gangbang and I would have gratefully consented, sucked the tall forwards dry twice and made them all pizza toast afterwards.

John called the engraved number and Champers' human directed us to her home, which was not far. We returned the suicidal animal to a grateful senior called Lucy who asked us in for oatmeal slice, and I wondered if you could call it a meet cute if you had already met on the internet.

I rushed John home. Eleven rubbed against his legs. Then I rubbed myself immediately against John, who was catnip and a friend to all cats, and he said, 'I don't think I'm sorry at all.'

It had been a while since I had properly kissed a person. The wife had lost interest in the practice years ago. The libertarian hadn't kissed me, and nor had Hayden. Anton the Russian had just squeezed my poonanny. Georges had sort of bitten my mouth recently, though he was a hot little fucker and would probably win most contests of Who Would You Rather? But John was the person who went to all the bother of kissing me.

'Whatever you want,' I said to him. 'Whatever you want, I'll do it.'

This may have been a more significant offer from one who was not queer, fond of anal, intensely interested in BDSM and a three-way graduate. I mean, I'll basically give anything consensual a go so long as it does not involve animals, underage persons or poo. The offer of 'whatever you want' to a shy straight man from the labour movement posed no real risk for me. I imagined that he'd ask me to wear suspender stockings, at most. Still, it felt quite hot and servant-girl to say it. *Whatever you want.*

'Well. I'd like a drink,' he said. Which was not so hot to hear.

There was no alcohol here. There had never been any alcohol here that lasted more than an evening. Bottles were emptied almost as soon as they arrived and rather than offer the history of my ex-wife's alcohol use, I decided, for the sake of my vagina, to not say anything pompous about the Twelve Steps at all. I would just pop across the road and ask Sally for a loaner and get the reasonably handsome prick a drink.

Sally should be a mandatory presence on every street. Some may regard her as the neighbourhood gossip; I like to think of her as our local historian. She knows everybody's name and their present states of housing equity and marriage. Last week she had seen me walk to Eleni's and she said, 'Oh darling. I'm sorry.' There was no need to ask 'How did you know that she left me?' Sally just always knows everything.

'Got company already? Good girl. Get a divorce, then back on the horse. Not a mare this time, I see,' she said.

'I was wondering if you had something cheap and nasty you could give me?' I said.

'I think we'll leave that to the badly dressed gentlemen. Ha ha ha. No. Really. Wear a condom. I've got some sangiovese left over from Christmas. It tastes like rat piss, but I guess it's not the only thing . . . ha ha ha . . . that does . . . ha.'

I reminded Sally that we all knew the Roadside Assistance van had been in her driveway *again* on New Year's Day for a length of time sufficient to charge twenty car batteries, and that if she didn't admit that she too was a dirty whore I would start a Facebook page called 'Sally the Whore Across the Road is Doing the Automobile Club Man Again'.

'Mechanics rev me up!' she said gaily and gave me two bottles of wine whose quality, she hoped, would be outshone by the poorly dressed gentleman as soon as he took off his awful clothes.

'Sorry,' said John, as he looked up from his iPhone. 'Sorry,' he said as I poured him a glass of bad wine.

I gave myself a splash, too. I did this partially out of good manners and partially out of the need for insulation. He no longer seemed present. I was pretty sure he had just been on a dating app—by now I was familiar with the colour and the mood of brown eyes just raised from an intimate screen.

But as proceeds the motto of the desperate and horny: first, you lower your standards, then, you lower your pants.

The standard-lowering drop of wine was not to my taste. John, however, drained his glass with the blithe thirst of an old-time working man. He took another wine and set it down halfway so he could talk about the thoughts of the Greek economist, Yanis Varoufakis, and then when he'd hit some sort of peak on monetary policy, he said, 'Whatever I want?'

'Are you going to ask for cheese and biscuits?' I said.

'I was going to ask you to come over here.'

Look. This dialogue was not one shade better than anything provided by *Fifty*. And this faltering night had started to get on my last effing nerve. When I was alone I knew I could expect to careen from desire to despair in an instant. I had held out a more constant hope for the influence of other people, and this John fellow seemed to flip from intimacy to unconcern faster than a cat. *He* hadn't just been left by his no-good girlfriend for a much younger woman or quit his hateful job. He was therefore obliged to act much better than me.

I didn't come over there. Instead I sat, exhausted, on my own chair.

'Yours is a pleasant home,' he said.

'Thanks.'

'This sofa is comfortable but chic,' he said.

'Hmn.'

'You have really remarkable tits.'

'I know,' I said, and he asked me to undress.

I said no.

Other than for purely comic purposes, I could never ritually disrobe for others. Striptease is best left to professionals, or at least to amateurs who have more rhythm than me. In general, I am about as rhythmic as gastroenteritis. I had also become pretty cranky.

I had also run out of economics conversation. I could either keep talking to this hyper-casually dressed member of the policy class and reveal the limits of my knowledge, or I could get my tits out.

I got my tits out. Comically, of course.

'Oh. Goodness gracious. It seems that my teeny little dress has fallen off while I was foraging for blackberries for Mother,' I said as I showed him my tits and my middle finger.

'Whatever can be done?' he said.

'And I, just a mere girl of forty-three. I do hope I'm not snared in the brambles! Or that some terrible menacing man doesn't come along and explain the danger of the overlooked relationship between monetary and fiscal settings in Europe again. Because that would be fucking boring, John, by which of course we mean totally sexy and hot.'

'Some beast who would threaten you with talk of public debt crisis? Some swarthy woodsman who would tell you to spend in a bust and frighten the dress right off you?!' said John, as he moved towards me.

'Yes, dude. Totally. Oh. Oh. Look at you. You are as big as the national debt of Portugal.'

'You are as hot as the tempers of communist Greeks,' he said.

I was enjoying myself again. I was laughing and had certainly picked up more basic knowledge on the role of the state in gearing economic cycles. This reminder of the superstructure would come in handy when arguing with my stupid neoliberal relatives again next Christmas.

He kissed me again and again; it was quite good. He did slobber a little and this was further enslobbened by his caution; every time he stopped kissing me, presumably to allow me to freely deny consent should I wish to, I felt the threads of saliva slowly break between our faces.

This guy needed help finding his way out of the policy class and into my vagina. It was frustrating that it fell to me, a person quite out of heterosexual practice, to take the lead. But not so frustrating that I wouldn't take it.

It was now a matter not just of horniness but one of pride that I should have something like proper, lying-down sex. More specifically, proper, lying-down sex with someone who had half a mind to objectify me. I needed to be objectified.

Whatever shiny rot the Barbie feminists have to say on the topic, objectification is crucial to the act of sex. Even those in a long, intimate marriage need their partner to desire them not at all for their inner life but for their bodies alone.

This is not to say at all that the other person's insides don't count. This moment of desire with John was produced by the fact that we mildly respected the other's insides. For all its flaws, this was the most genuine intimacy I'd shared in years and it could not have been enacted with anyone but a Marxist—which he was, despite all the Neo-Keynesian pillow talk.

But there's a point when you need to cast away all the things that brought you together and just fuck each other as distant objects. I needed to push him towards that detachment.

'You're so hard,' I said into his ear and, yes, of course I am aware that this is the remark of a hack. But, notwithstanding our revulsion for standard speech, the plain fact is, 'you're so hard' continues to be an effective means of making a man forget himself. Follow this with a fairly breathy, 'So. Fucking. Hard', and even the policy worker trained in sexual discrimination safeguards will forget to ask you if it's okay if he can grab your arse and will, *finally*, just grab your arse.

I kissed the anterior triangle of a neck that I had so recently found creepy. These curiously over-worked muscles no longer signified danger but simply gave me hope that he had sufficient upper body strength to fuck me good and proper. When I had not been imagining edge-play with masked men, I had been thinking that a wholesome missionary thrashing was something I had experienced only so rarely and so very long ago that it would now seem as perverse as a public flogging.

It did.

This straight sex felt so bent to me. I'm pretty sure it didn't feel at all bent to John, who had smiled untroubled throughout.

I didn't ask for or do anything pushy or peculiar. That is, if we do not count my insistence on rubber-free sex.

> **Public Service Announcement:** There can be no justification at all for the wilful shunning of condoms. Put your love in a glove, etc. Even if, like me, you came to sexual maturity in the nineties when the failure to use a condom was so forbidden, it would remain irresistible to you for years. Perhaps if you hate the stupid franger as much as I do, you should consider devoting the rest of your waking life to prophylactic technologies and produce a material that doesn't smell of cheap sports stores and doesn't make a perfectly reasonably cock feel like a polyp. Please. Do this for humanity.

There are those who will say with great confidence that 'she really knows how to fuck' or 'he's fantastic in bed'. I don't know what instruments these persons have at their disposal or how they would calibrate them to assess the merits of a particular sexual actor. I do know, however, that I quite enjoyed myself.

I also know that if I had not been so receptive to pleasure this could have been some terrible sex. Which is something, of course, you can say about all sex, but I couldn't shake the sense that John's pleasure was entirely contingent on mine.

I know this *sounds* nice. I know people, most especially female ones, often describe their ideal sexual partner as one who gets off on their other's delight. But lopsided devotion to my pleasure always makes me feel like a bit of a rapist. I've never liked another person's total eagerness to serve.

Years before, I had lived in a lesbian separatist household. The young women who live in lesbian separatist households are, for reasons of hormones and convenience, very likely to have sex with all the other occupants at some point. So one night I was invited into the bed of a med student called Sherri, who happened to be unspeakably hot.

When I set upon this lovely brown body it lay, mostly, inert. She screwed her eyes up not with elation, but with disgust. When it became clear that I would continue to fail to serve her Sherri began serving me. She said, 'You're really enjoying yourself, baby, aren't you?' so often that I came very close to not coming.

As I've mentioned, such a lapse has rarely occurred. I come often and easily. Even when the object of something close to hatred. But this climax, and the exchange that had preceded it, wasn't much chop.

After I'd come, she cried. I asked her what was wrong and she said, 'I'm worried about my Clinical Skills exam,' which was obvious bullshit. She was, I think, unhappy about giving everything and not getting anything in return. Even though she'd insisted on these terms.

Not that John was crying, and not that he hadn't quite happily received my second ever full-service blow job. Not that he hadn't said, at least a dozen times, 'That was fucking insane.' Not that he hadn't gone for seconds and thirds and forgotten to drink Sally's bad wine for at least half an hour.

But he did seem not only sensitive to my needs but dependent on them. He seemed to have a need for the needy.

It wasn't too much trouble providing this delusion. I found that whimpering a bit and looking tearful and saying 'I need your cock' got him aroused to the point where he was no longer thinking about my needs and went on to develop and fulfil his own.

It was a bit more trouble for me to seem needy in conversation. Which is peculiar because I don't think I've ever been quite so emotionally needy in all my adult life. But no one who talks as much opinionated shit as I do could ever be apprehended as needy. Boring, loud or misguided, perhaps. But never needy.

As we lay awake all night talking opinionated shit, he said a few times that he thought I was very strong. Very independent. Very sure of myself. I did nothing to correct this perception.

He went to smoke a cig out the back, and when he returned to my side he asked if I was an artist.

'Fuck no, John. I'm a cut-price copywriter. Whatever gave you that idea?'

'Well, I just saw a lot of art materials out in the back shed.'

'Oh. Right. Those. They're not mine.'

'Oh, okay,' he said, and even though he would have left it at that, I decided to tell him a truth-lie hybrid because, damn it, I quite liked him now and I certainly didn't want him suspecting me of found-object sculpture.

'I have an ex. She left, um, about six months ago and hasn't moved her shit out yet.'

John worked in politics and had developed a good poker face for the game. But, he was a bit drunk and wearing only his underpants at 4 a.m., so the mask of indifference had dropped a bit.

'*She* left,' he said, and then looked embarrassed when he realised he'd emphasised a word that he shouldn't. He was surprised, but possibly not aroused, to learn I had been a lezzer.

'I mean, she *left*,' he said. 'I mean, why would anyone leave you, a citizen gifted of such excellent tits?'

'I don't know, John. Possibly something to do with all those forty-something Marxist men I lured into the house, drugged and shipped to Goldman Sachs for economic reprogramming. The bitch was afraid of hard work.'

'Well, this is embarrassing,' he said. 'Here was I thinking you'd be worth a good twenty grand when I sold you off to Chevron to be retrained as a professional corporate apologist for oil spills.'

We talked sleepy bunkum for a while, and when the sun resumed its plan to fade the curtains, he identified all the birdsong we could hear. Then he said, 'I like you and your cat and your smart mouth a lot,' and continued to like these things quite well until the end of summer.

When he was here, I refused to sleep, and when he was not, I couldn't. Damn Rumi for making me confuse sleep-deprivation with affection! There really is quite a difference.

John equals five dates as per my earlier stipulation, therefore thirty-six down and sixty-four dates remaining.

23

Half a season since she left

So Rumi apologised personally. Then Jesus wept and Karl Marx cried from his grave in London when what instruments they had agreed: things are pretty crap for Helen.

Let me try to serve this shit to you quickly enough that you won't have a chance to say, 'Bitch, I told you so.'

I learned that John had been seeing several other ladies. Not that he said that he would not, but (a) he hadn't said that he *would*, and (b) the condom problem.

After I had been rogering John for a week or so, I got a hold of my ridiculous dolphin and had a grown-up chat with her. I had requested a full sexual health check from my doctor and I had asked John if he would do the same so that we could continue with our 'unprotected sex'.

Which is a phrase that had always given me the irrits for its insinuation that there could ever be such a thing as 'protected sex' which there clearly can't because people just seem to go about destroying the memory of the sex they had with you by making you cry and cry.

Anyhow, John had consented to the test and said that he had received a good report and I had no reason to doubt that his was not an organ uncontaminated until some dirty lady started 'liking' all of his posts on Facebook and writing 'lol' beneath them.

When I asked, which I did immediately after she'd typed a 'lol luv u', he said that he *was* 'seeing' her. And maybe some other lolling internet ladies as well. And, well, yes, he was sorry if he had compromised the integrity of our agreed sexual health defences, but I seemed so strong and independent he didn't think I'd mind about the actual non-monogamy.

To this I had to say, 'Well I don't mind about that part of it at all,' even though I very much did. And then, like a dick, I demanded to see him. We had sex twice on the cream L-shaped sofa in his lifeless flat, and I cried and I said, 'We can't do this again,' and he said, 'I know, but I love you.'

I said, 'I love you, too,' and I have absolutely no notion how to explain this exchange. Other than to say it reminded me, again, of *1984*. Specifically, that part after Julia and Winston have been released from Room 101.

Following their imprisonment, the lovers meet again. They have given each other up to the cruel fascists of Ingsoc after days of torture conditions.

'I betrayed you,' she said baldly.
'I betrayed you,' he said.

'I love you' should probably not feel as though it were coaxed from you by a pack of hungry rats; as though you were tormented into saying it and that now love was itself the betrayal.

We continued making this declaration to each other daily for a month. It never felt particularly good. It felt like a dreadful confession. Once I got nearly as drunk as he was every night by 9 p.m. and I called him and demanded to know 'What the fuck do you *mean*, "I love you"?'

He said that it meant he found me very difficult.

I said that he could eat my difficult shit.

He said, after I had been nagging for half an hour or so, 'It means that I love you so much, I can't be with you.'

I told him that I had NEVER fucking asked to be with him and he said that THIS was part of the problem.

I don't think the conversation that followed, which was, you must remember, produced by two vain people inclined to think they can talk in Charles Bukowski stanzas just because they've had that much to drink, deserves any further report.

We saw each other once again to 'work it out' and we worked nothing out at all, save for his acknowledgement that he was embarrassed by me socially. We had attended a handful of gatherings together, always those of my circle and never his, and, yes, I had told a silly lawyer once that same-sex marriage was not true equality but equality under the law and should be shunned. I had argued with someone else about the futility of awareness ribbons. And I had told an inspiring liberal feminist that she only cared about diversity on boards, not wealth for all the people and, fuck, he agreed with this stuff. He just didn't want it spoken.

'You argue with people all the time about politics, Helen.'

'But you argue with people about politics for a living!' I said.

'That's the point. I'm *paid* to do it.'

I growled at him about how the revolution was hardly going to happen inside office hours and, ahem, *given* that his most recent policy project sought to assess all the unpaid labour performed by women, he should start by counting mine.

He told me again that he loved me. I said that I loved him, too.

He had tried to pick up my friend and hairstylist, April, who we'd run into that night at the pub. When I'd got up to buy both of them a drink, he'd said to her, 'If I can get rid of her, would you like to come back to my place?'

April is a decent person and so told me this immediately. She is also a polyamorous person but she would never (a) fuck someone who dressed that badly and smelled that much of sausage, and (b) consent to a non-poly invitation, which John's had been.

If I can get rid of her. This was an invitation to not just fuck but to fuck me up.

I'm certain he did want sex with April. Everyone, including myself, has tried to have sex with April. She has legs as long as an opera and looks like Grace Kelly might have if she'd traded the soft life of a Grimaldi for a punishing program of kettlebells. She is also funny, and once, when explaining her polyamory to me, said, 'Helen. It's just that I love that new dick smell.'

I'm absolutely sure he really did want to boff her. Everybody does. But he longed to embarrass me more.

I would like to tell you that at this point I never again spoke with a man who seemed only to tell me that he loved me, and then hear it in return, so he could defile those declarations moments later.

He sent me an official looking letter next day by courier. It had 'SORRY' diagonally stamped on it.

> When I woke this morning and remembered what I'd done, I was stunned and unbelieving. It could only be the work of some fearful, loathing, intoxicated monster that I didn't recognise as myself. Now I do.
>
> Fuck.
>
> The fact that my stink contaminated your life; that my degradation violated this wonderful person and her friendship, sickens me. It is unforgivable, but I am asking for your forgiveness.
>
> Why should you provide it? I really don't know.
>
> I know that that I am not a twat 100 per cent of the time, or that at least some of the time my cuntiness is

not observable and harmless. Why do I act that way? I don't know and I can't guarantee that it won't happen again. I think I was improving and I will continue to work on it.

I know that the haughty little two-person club we formed was a useful and fun place to be. I know that your opinions and feelings matter to me. I know you are SOUND. I know this is a pathetic note and about as effective as an official government apology. However, unlike official government apologies, there will be some action to back up the symbolism. Here is a graph showing declining levels of cuntiness over the forecast period.

Gradients of 'actual, estimated and projected cuntiness' were shown across a one-year period. These made me laugh and I forgave him, because who doesn't need a friend who is handy with a line graph?

*

I resumed my dating project. I met an internet man named Ayaan who did not believe in sex before marriage. Thirty-eight down. I saw a chap called Reid who I had met thanks to an associate. He was too hopeful and contented for my taste. Sixty-one to go. We had argued about the effectiveness of Awareness campaigns and ate garlic squid rings, which reminded me to bump up my lady numbers. To that end, I arranged to see an old university girlfriend, Sophie.

We agreed about nearly everything and it was fucking awesome to see this super-bright, angry dyke after so long, but she was married, which I'd neglected to ask in advance, but, still, forty down.

I made plans with Ines, the sleepwear designer friend of Maddie's, and I let John know what I had been doing. I thought how good it was that he had become such a dependable old friend in such a short time. I thought that it was nice that he still sometimes phoned to say that he loved me. It felt fine to say it in return.

He had said the Helen One Hundred was hilarious and asked me to keep him updated. I told him that I was thinking about recording this stuff and that I might write down an account of our Winston/Julia thing, and he said he didn't mind much.

On my blog, I wrote a long and fairly fawning piece about how hard he had made me come. It wasn't quite the worst thing I have ever written, but it was certainly the most emotionally senile. Anyhow, this post had revealed a single identifying detail, since removed, to a single reader who contacted me to tell me that she had had a coinstantaneous relationship with John.

We ended up talking on the phone. She said his *sort-of* cheating hadn't surprised her. She wasn't surprised by the fact that he had also broken out the birdsong trick to her the first morning after all-night sex, either—although she was surprised that a guy who ate so many sausages had so much energy.

The thing that was really troubling her was the possibility that he'd told me that he loved me.

I said that he had, but only after we'd broken the stupid thing off. The same thing had happened to her, she said. They were still friends and she really depended on him as the emotional background to her regular life. He wanted regular updates. He said that he loved her, but that he couldn't be with her because he loved her too much.

Now it may be the case that John genuinely felt this way about several women he had dumped at once. I do understand that it is possible for people to feel this kind of love. But that does not make it endurable to receive.

I rang John at work and I gave him what for and I said that I didn't care if he had an important meeting about the unpaid work of my gender because if he really wanted to do something for women, he would fucking stop fucking messing with our fucking woman heads.

I went on for an unnecessarily long time. I said that I hoped that I had ruined his day. He said that I had. I said *good* and I asked him for four hundred dollars. This, I explained, would cover four sessions with Gerard, which were much needed to undo these months of psychological hijinks.

'But, remember. I only need four,' I said. 'You're a right prick. But you're the kind of prick I can recover from in four 45-minute sessions. All of which will be with Cheap Gerard. Who is not even particularly good.'

John transferred the sum that day.

THE HELEN 100

I do not know, but I do suspect that John, who honours his debts, did not continue to be a right prick. It was a hot summer and people were going batty left and right. There was a dry and spiteful northerly blowing into town most days and no one of my acquaintance was at rights.

Certainly, the heat had affected the ex. New life was brought to Gerard's business that terrible season, but the rest of us were just stuck by the heat in old themes.

By the time the weather had cooled she had come by to take most of her stuff. Eleven seemed exhausted, but he had been wearing such a great tabby coat.

I did manage to expunge the John damage with Gerard. Actually, it took just one session during which Gerard smoked and said, 'He sounds like a bit of a fuckwit,' in slightly different ways. He did encourage me to try to take something good from the dead friendship and then immediately apologised for this upbeat suggestion. 'Look. I have all these new clients who seem to want positive thinking exercises,' he explained.

I thought that John had given me two good reminders. The first was to take better care of my genital health. The second was that I was *not* paid to argue politics.

After years of writing sales tripe and several months of writing nothing profitable at all, I decided that I would like to be paid to argue politics. I found some work with some papers. It didn't make me wealthy, but it did permit me to bang on about Marx and demanded that I did so with some recourse to a fucking clue.

I remained, of course, a miserable abhorrence. I cried and engaged in obsessive behaviours and began to run irrationally long distances and rarely bothered to eat.

'This is what I have to deal with now,' I said in her shed, which was finally emptied.

24

One new sleeping garment

Ines is magnificent. No, really. I know I tend to mistreat adjectives and have mistreated them for several chapters—this, I believe, is the result of several years composing lies for discount advertising firms. But be assured, this adjective is judiciously applied.

If you met Ines or saw her even from a distance, as you are bound to if you visit a fashionable Melbourne bar, you would say, 'Razer really got it right for once. Ines *is* actually magnificent.'

It was now early autumn and I had known Ines a little for a long time before we met that night on Spring Street. For years, we had been invited to the same places by the same homosexuals who introduced us at least a dozen times with 'I just know you two whores will adore each other!'

On the second or third of these occasions, she retorted, 'You know, I really don't think we will.' On the fourth or fifth, Ines, a famous Top, had said, 'No, incorrect. Two doms don't make a right.'

She may have been misled about my power preference, which is, as I think I have amply explained, submissive. Nonetheless, this misunderstanding led to a funny line. She was full of funny lines and she was also very glamorous. As an envious sort of person, I could only tolerate this combination of glamour and comedy in the dead. No magnificent woman had any business cracking it like Dorothy Parker while I was still alive.

I had resented Ines's beauty, her shoes and her basically mystic arse. She had taught her arse to wiggle independent of gravity, space and time. When she walks across a room—and she does this often—her arse keeps a rhythm of its own. I suspect her of slightly shaving the heel of one of her shoes, as Marilyn Monroe once did. And I know that any reference to this well-documented wiggle is risky. But go to a fashionable Melbourne bar and wait for Ines's superior shake to confuse you into buying all of her evening's shiraz. You'll see that the comparison is fair.

We'd never liked each other. Not one jot. I'd *like* to tell you this was because we were just two alpha bitches who were too evenly matched. But I *have* to tell you it was because I was jealous and unhappy that I was not as free as Ines. I was, as a result, always unpleasant when we met.

Quite justifiably, she would not have consented to meet me again now if I hadn't written first to apologise that I'd been such a vile heifer. She replied, 'Darling, I never knew you could be such a ma-a-a-rvellous sap.'

Ines had the sort of fastidious commitment to camp expression that permits her moments of unusual sincerity. This is the ma-a-a-rvellous thing about truly quality camp. If you routinely treat life with a pair of disposable gloves on and refuse to take too much of it too seriously, every so often you can touch it deeply. A life lived in artifice means you can more easily be emotionally naked, sort of thing.

Ines is *actually* naked often. She is banned from Facebook weekly for her full-frontal display. There is never a time when she is not involved in an ardent correspondence with Silicon Valley wherein she holds that her nudity is not true nudity but a ma-a-a-rvellous performance of femininity, and one that is not intended to offend but simply to lift people's spirits. Which it does, particularly in her series of naked portraits taken at a Gilbert & George retrospective, where she, somehow, managed to escape arrest while dry humping the artists' most valuable canvas.

When you meet her, the first thing she will tell you, *sotto voce*, is, 'Darling. I was raised by drag queens.' Plenty of profoundly camp people say this to explain their outfits, but in Ines's case it happens to be true. When she was quite young, she found work in a brothel that was managed by a particularly maternal drag queen.

There she studied both the trade of the sex worker and advanced camp living. I think this glitz preserved the sweetness of the little girl in her because she was able to hold my hand when we met for the first time as allies and say, 'I know how you are feeling. Like you'll never feel the sun on your skin.' Which is pretty spot on, as we dumped people know.

Ines has a lisp—of course she does—so the noise she actually made was more like, 'the thun on your thkin'. The slight and persistent shift from everyday elocution only served to make the sincere things she said sound even more sincere.

Ines is *magnificent*.

We were able to talk at length about the queer shame of a break-up. When I mentioned to Ines how so many progressive people seemed particularly affronted that I had let a same-sex relationship fail, she said she knew exactly what I meant.

'When I ended things with that last long-term lunatic, everybody was saying, "What a shame, what a shame." As though it were my legal fucking obligation to remain in a pit of despair with an unfashionable lesbian who was cruel and vindictive and more full of drugs than a pharmacy,' she said.

'Everybody who is not one's mother is deeply disappointed,' I said.

'Do you know what I ab-so-lute-ly loathe?' she asked.

'People who don't look at your arse when you waggle it across the room?'

'Oooh. Cheeky. Well, obviously that. Who are these people and can we get them some government spectacles? No.

Apart from those Magoos who will never know the pleasure of my ma-a-a-rvellous trunk due to social injustice, it's my mother who I loathe. For several reasons, which start but do not end with the theft of my childhood, but the one I mean now is for how *thrilled* she always is when she learns I have slept with a man.'

Some conservative folks are happy when a lez lady goes back on solids. And then, of course, the reverse with feminist friends, even and especially the straight ones, who seemed disturbed by my quest to locate a penis and then almost happy that the penis that I had managed to locate was attached to someone who had treated me cruelly. It was all very I Told You So.

'Everyone disapproves. Of everything, generally. Is it any wonder that everyone here is dressed so poorly, what with all that disapproval getting in the way of good costume? And I am sorry to say, dear, that you're one of those bad dressers. As you've plainly been on the ma-a-a-rvellous eat-nothing-but-your-own-bitter-tears divorce diet, this is a waste of a waist.'

Ines always has somewhere else to be and tonight she was preparing for some act of high-end nudity on the north side of the river. But we both agreed it had been a lovely evening and she said, 'If you promise to dress better next time, I will probably kiss you.'

The following day, I received a gift with uncommon wrapping. In a box that had been—I don't know the word, you'd have to ask Ines—appliquéd (?) with quotes from Dotty Parker, there was a lovely dress.

'My Dear and Unfashionable Friend,' said the note:

Here's a little something I designed. You can wear it when next we meet or you can save it for a man you have first carefully assessed for his dress-removing aptitude. Don't wear it for a disapproving lesbian. She'll never understand. Whatever you do and however you dress, please, you dizzy bitch, try to remember that Marxism is fine in a lover but kindness is much better. Gros Bisous!

Forty-one down.
Thirty-nine to go.
One new friend, who I treasure.

25

Some months, six kilograms of kindness

I have spent more time with Eleven the cat than any other being. As I sat at my desk and wrote rotten things for money, there he was. As I returned late at night from the hospital where my ex was moving to a paralysing diagnosis, there he was. As I lay on the floor crying about counterfeit love and listening for the sound of something real in my stupid, big girl sobs, there he was.

Eleven was made from stripes and from sweetness. He was unique and aggressively affectionate. He reminded me for ten years of the possibility of mutual kindness.

Eleven had seemed off his game that summer. By March, he was off his food. I attributed this to the loss of his other human. Then, when I visited the vet, I found that it was down to something even more unmanageable. My little guy had a stomach cancer.

When I first met him at the shelter—when he was not called Eleven but 'Surrender from Scoresby'—he was an adult cat so eager to love that he knocked me over with the force of his snout. He loved to ram things that way.

There are behavioural explanations for this snout rubbing performed by cats, which is properly known as 'bunting'. None describes the gratitude I felt when the little guy seemed to stop just short of injuring me with his kindness.

You may think I'm a mad cat lady who ascribes human emotion to a face biologically unable to convey anything more nuanced than hunger or fear, but that's just because you haven't looked into those sofa-green eyes. They showed me kindness.

They saved me and sustained me and helped me know that love is not always a fake. They made me believe I could see a flicker of it in a human. If it had not been for Eleven, I would have been doomed to miss this look of love. I would probably have mistaken it for indigestion.

If someone was ever able to love me to an Eleven standard, I knew what to look for.

The vet answered all my questions and assured me that this tumour had nothing to do with barbecue chicken. He was a kind and rational man. His evidence-based approach was matched with great sensitivity. He and I and the pathology lab made the decision to kill Eleven. And we made it with kindness.

THE HELEN 100

Because kindness is the only thing that matters, I reluctantly allowed as my cat died in my arms.

Don't tell the Marxists I said that.

But you can totally tell your cat.

26

They never really leave, do they?
I was cold and I was lonely and my cat was fucking dead. I had missed out on the opportunity to partake of Ines's naked magnificence because I had been crying for my dead cat.

Also, the six dates I'd endured after that were sad bullshit— I'd struck a run of others also recovering from a midlife break-up. Also, the walnut tree had died, and I had heard the ex was happy and in love.

On the upside, I *had* (a) read and understood most of *Capital Volume 1*, (b) retained my girlish break-up figure and (c) run a marathon, albeit at geriatric pace.

On balance, I was tolerably miserable. I was yet to feel sun on my skin, but confident that winter could not kill me.

I said to myself that I did not mourn my youth. I looked in the mirror and sometimes managed to make myself feel grateful to have lived long enough to acquire such dull skin. I flossed my teeth, I washed my sheets, and I exchanged my time and thought for money.

I believed that I had become patient and moderate and slow. I was a slow, moderate, patient lady who had no need to run. Except when in training for some midlife runners' event.

I cannot be sure what it was about Date 53 that restored a sense of speed. It's not as though he were fast at all.

Although he was quite a bit younger than me and had much longer legs, he was awfully deliberate and slow. I noticed when I met him how careful he was about everything. He paid for our coffee carefully. He returned the change to his wallet carefully. He carefully offered his services free-of-charge as a careful proofreader for my sometimes reckless work.

'You know, I really do enjoy your cranky pinko bleating, but I think it might be improved if you learn how to use the semicolon. I make this offer purely as a self-interested reader,' he said, and then he smiled.

If he hadn't had eyes bluer and more cheerful than a box of laundry detergent, I might have felt insulted. If he hadn't spoken these words in a soft but ovary-shaking baritone, I might have said, 'Fuck you, I know how to use a semicolon.'

Then again, if he hadn't been six foot five and handsome and an old-school Marxist curiously besotted with the utterance of grammatically spotless sentences, I wouldn't have had one of my high-speed tantrums about nothing. Which was, in this case, about the fact that he hadn't walked me home after such a nice, long time together. Even though I had explicitly insisted that he mustn't.

And I wouldn't have belted him with three days of angry emails, none of which make any sense to me now, but all of which contained, as he later pointed out, one correctly placed semicolon.

We continued to meet and I continued to pick fights that had as their topic some imaginary mortification or, when I couldn't find a conversational fault line big enough to take a shit in, the fact, the *terrible* fact, that *eleven years* had elapsed between our birthdates.

One day, I met him at the movies. I arrived to see him sitting on a couch. He said that he was *not* untroubled by my faithful fifteen minutes of lateness. He said that he was truly tired of waiting. He said that he did not care to wait any longer.

I said that he would not wait again.

And, you know, I *would* go into detail. I *would* tell you that I am now content and sane and that I have truly 'grown'. But who needs that hopeful flapdoodle? Only liars and cheats. What *you* need is just one mild truth: you'll never get over your fucking divorce. But you will learn to do things differently.

In the end, Cheap Gerard was right.